George Veal

Musical travels through England

George Veal

Musical travels through England

ISBN/EAN: 9783743314023

Manufactured in Europe, USA, Canada, Australia, Japa

Cover: Foto ©Thomas Meinert / pixelio.de

Manufactured and distributed by brebook publishing software (www.brebook.com)

George Veal

Musical travels through England

TO THE

GOVERNORS and GUARDIANS of the HOSPITAL for the Maintenance and Education of exposed and deserted young Children.

GENTLEMEN,

*W*HILE *I was extracting the following sheets from my Journal, as a Specimen of my laborious investigation of the present state of* MUSIC *in this country, I was somewhat at a loss to whom I could with most propriety inscribe my work. Whether to* DOCTOR BURNEY, *as the original inventor of this species of composition, and the first musical traveller of our nation, of whom I might so truly say in his own words,* " *that he has long been my* magnus Apollo:" —*or to the King of* Prussia, *as the greatest* Dilettante *performer of the age; who, like another* Nero, *is playing his new* Solfeggi *to the groans of the miserable* Poles, *and ruined* Dantzickers. *This dilemma, however,*

ever, was at an end, as soon as I learnt that Dr. Burney, *and Signor* Giardini, *had, under your authority, and in imitation of the* Italian confevatorrios, *juſt founded a ſchool for muſic in the* FOUNDLING HOSPITAL, *where deſerted orphans, inſtead of being placed out to trades and ſervices, in which they can have no opportunity of making any* noiſe *in the world, are, in future, to be trained to harmony from their infancy, and conſtantly employed in the ſtudy of the ſcience of ſound, till in proceſs of time they take their regular degrees in muſic, and fill all our public orcheſtras with* Engliſh *Giardinis and* Baſtardinis dette Ingliſene. *When I was informed of this important event, I hailed the happy omen, the dawn of an* Auguſtan æra; *and reſolved to dedicate my work to a ſet of gentlemen, who have ſhewn ſo diſtinguiſhed a zeal for the intereſt and advancement of muſic.*

Perhaps it may at firſt appear a bold undertaking in the guardians of expoſed and deſerted children, who are chiefly ſupported by parliamentary grants of public money, to declare, that they cannot be maintained

tained by the public for a more useful purpose, than to be taught to sing and play. For men of narrow and contracted minds, who have neither ear, nor voice, nor hand, will still imagine, that it might prove of more national utility, to breed these adopted children of the public, to Husbandry, Navigation, &c. the objects of their original destination; than to convert one of the noblest of our public charities into a nursery for the supply of musical performers at our Theatres, gardens, and hops.---But this is a vulgar prejudice. The improvement of the fine arts ought to be the first object of public attention in an age of luxury, peace, and plenty, like the present. When we have rivalled the Italians in music, it will be time enough to think of our Navy, and our Agriculture. We have already (to our shame be it spoken) more sailors than singers, and better farmers than fiddlers. But as I take this circumstance to arise entirely from the different degree of encouragement these occupations have hitherto received; I do not despair of seeing the reverse take place, when gentlemen of your rank deign to stand forward, and by the influence and
sanction

sanction of their example, correct the errors of the vulgar. Should any *obstacle arise to impede the immediate execution of your plan, from some obsolete but unrepealed parliamentary restrictions, doubtless the same legislators who so readily expended the public money in the purchase of* Sir William Hamilton's collection *of antique vases, and* Etruscan *rarities, and enacted a lottery for toys, will repeal any former act which may stand in your way; and as they must rejoice in a fresh opportunity of displaying their fine taste and love of the arts, I am not without hope that the first act of this present session will be intitled* An Act for instituting a musical academy in the Foundling-Hospital, *and for raising a competent sum for the purchase of the best* Cremonas, and other instruments which can be procured on the continent, for the service thereof. *This would be opening the new parliament with an* eclat *that would astonish all Europe, and make the King of* Prussia, *and all the fiddling Electors of Germany die with envy. I have only to add, gentlemen, that if upon a perusal of the following sheets, you should find, as I*

am

am perfuaded you will, that my travels are also * in fome meafure, a matter of national concern; I hope you will be kind enough to fecond my intended application to the Houfe of Commons, that the charges of my future expeditions may be defrayed at the public expence. This may be done by a very fhort claufe in the fame act; and as it will enable me to purfue my enquiries with greater fpirit and credit, will lay a lafting obligation upon,

Gentlemen,

Your very obedient,

and devoted humble Servant,

JOEL COLLIER.

---

* —" He was the firft who feemed to think my journey " was, in fome meafure, a matter of national concern."
TOUR THROUGH GERMANY, &c.

Speedily will be published,

An Enquiry into the Present State

OF THE

MUSIC OF THE SPHERES.

By JOEL COLLIER, Licentiate in Music.

*Avia Pieridum perago loca nullius ante
Trita solo.* LUCR.

*Into the heav'n of heav'ns I have presum'd,
An earthly guest, and* stol'n *empyrean* tunes. MILT.

☞ Many superficial critics having been pleased to treat the notion of a celestial orchestra with the contempt due to the projectors of a philosopher's stone, a perpetual motion, or a lottery calculation, the author begs leave to assure the *connocenti* that he has not proceeded in his enquiries without sufficient *data*. He has made very accurate observations upon the sound of thunder, considered as the *thorough-bass* of " all " heaven's harmonies." He has likewise studied and compared the different motions of the planets in their periodical country-dances and cotillons; as described by the orrery. He appeals therefore as well to Doctors as Under-graduates in the profession, whether it is not possible even for " *musicians of this nether world,*" to ascertain the measure of a dance by the motions of the performers?—And when once the thorough-bass of a concert is known, to find out the other parts of it by analogy?

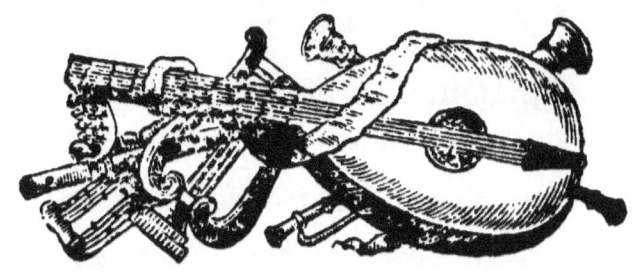

MUSICAL TRAVELS, &c.

I WAS born in the Parish of *Gotham*, in the county of *Nottingham*: my father was a sawyer, and my mother had, for many years before her marriage, cried oysters and Newcastle-salmon about the streets of London. Neither of them are said to have been remarkable for their vocal or instrumental talents. My mother's voice was, indeed, exceedingly shrill and dissonant, as I have been credibly informed by the neighbours; however, I was no sooner born than I gave proofs of uncommon mufical propenfities. I entered the world, finging, inftead of crying; at leaft, my fquall was truly melodious, and ravifhed the ears of the midwife; tho', I muft confefs, the envious old hag of a nurfe did pretend that my mother and Mrs. *Midnight* miftook the origin of the wild notes I uttered as foon as I faw the light; and, infifting that they only denoted the wind-cholic, immediately drenched me with a large dofe of rhubarb: however, fhe has fince candidly owned, that fhe eafily fang me to fleep whenever I was peevifh, and that even by means of fuch fimple melody as *Jack Sprat,* or *hey diddle diddle, the cat and the fiddle.* A harfh and menacing recitative would as effectually deter me from a naughty trick, as a good whipping. The found of a drum, or any other martial mufic, had fuch an immediate effect upon my nerves, that I was always obliged to be turned dry before the piece was half over. The famous MARCH *in Saul* is too powerful for

me

me even at this day, tho' I can stand any other, without being offensive. Indeed, I am so well convinced of the connection between the sound and the sense in all good music, that I will venture to prescribe *Handel's water-piece*, and *Water parted from the sea*, as specifics for a strangury. There is great truth in what *Shakespeare* says of the bagpipe; and I have observed that a jockey always whistles to his horse upon these occasions, which never fails to produce great effects, tho' the performer want mouth ever so much.

One of the first circumstances I myself can recollect in my early years, was the great pleasure I took in hearing a blind boy play tunes on a bladder of air press'd between a bow-stick and its string. The Jew's-harp next engaged my attention; and afterwards the bag-pipe, barrel-organ and bassoon. Indeed I do remember having been told by my Grandmother, that whilst I was yet in coats, I took vast delight in pinching the tails of the Parson's litter of pigs, and would listen to their various notes and tones from the *f* sharp of the whine of the least of the family, quite down to the *b* flat grunt of the old boar himself. This, with my attention to my coral and bells, and rattle, singing thro' a comb and brown paper, together with the great expertness I afterwards shew'd in making whistles of reeds, and the recent bark of sycamore twigs, made the oldest people of the parish foretel, that I should one day or other become a great and celebrated Musician.

My taste for the sister art of music, Poetry, was likewise, as I am inform'd, observed very early in my childhood; as I always held my mouth wide open, when the Psalm was sung at our Parish-Church; and soon was able to repeat without book a great part of *Sternhold* and *Hopkins*'s excellent version of that great *Dilettante* performer on the harp,—King *Davia*'s pieces.

Having

Having been well inform'd that the infancy, and indeed the riper years of the great Doctor BURNEY passed in much the same manner, and with similar expectations from all the old ladies of his acquaintance; and having observed with what *eclat*, and indeed universal approbation of all people of taste, his ingenious account of his travels has been received, I conceived a design of following so illustrious an example, and travelling through the dominions of *England, Scotland* and *Ireland*, with the town of *Berwick* upon *Tweed*, to give the world a true state of the musical improvement and progression in these kingdoms; and hope I may flatter myself, that the Dr. himself will applaud my undertaking, and consider it as a proper supplement to his elaborate work.

Before I set forward on my travels, I chose to change my name from *Collier* to *Coglioni* or *Collioni*, as more euphonious; and on the first of April, having torn myself from the arms of my weeping wife,

wife, and four small children, I put my bassoon into a green-bag, and slung it across my shoulders; my large violoncello was laid on my knee as I sat in the waggon, and my clothes, with a bottle of brandy and some biscuits, were pack'd up in the viol-case. As I was neither patronized, nor franked on my tour by any Dilettante Lord *, I must confess the low state of my circumstances, and the poverty in which I had left my family, cast a damp on my spirits; but this was always soon dissipated by an air on the violoncello, and by recollecting the great advantage my travels, to enquire into the state of music in this island, would be of to my dear native country, and the fame and glory I should acquire by the publication

* Since my first edition a noble Lord in administration, and the best kettle-drummer in Europe, has furnished me with recommendatory letters to most of the custom-house officers and excisemen in the kingdom; so that I cannot fail hereafter of being introduced into the best company wherever I go.

of

of my work, perhaps only inferior to that of the great Dr. B. himself.

> Inspir'd by taste, o'er lands and seas HE flew,
> Europe he saw, and Europe saw him too.
> Thro' lands of singing, or of dancing slaves,
> Love-echoing woods, and lute-resounding waves.
> O while along the stream of time, that name
> Expanded flies, and gathers all its fame;
> Say, shall my little bark attendant sail,
> Pursue the triumph and partake the gale?—
> POPE.

Thus occasionally consoling myself, the waggon arrived at the famous and ancient city of

LINCOLN.

My first visit was to a young lady of high musical acquirements. She received me with a most bewitching air, which she sang to her guittar, for she had heard of my fame at *Gotham*, and was not unapprized of my ambulatory design: her name was originally *Fernihough*, but she had long dropped the *hough* at the end of it, as gothic and inharmonious. Thus she saluted me:

" Dear

" Dear Collioni, Collioni,
" Dear, dear, dear, Collioni;
" Happy, happy, happy Gotham;
" Gotham, Gotham, happy Gotham."

I could only bow and smile in answer to this compliment, (which, indeed, tho' very elegant, I did not conceive was above my merits,) as I had not an extempore sonnet ready made to answer it.

Then taking my hand with a delightful air, she introduced me to Dr. *Dilettanti*, a most illustrious timeist; he sat musing and beating the floor with his foot, and took hold of, and quitted my hand in the same portion of time, which he marked by the pulsations of his foot.

" Excuse, said he, illustrious *Collioni*,
" the measured mode of my gestures in
" saluting you; but I have long ac-
" customed myself to measure out the parts
" of time on a variety of sounding instru-
" ments, and have at length introduced it
" into all the motions of my body. At
" my house, sir, you will learn to cut your
" meat,

"meat, and move your jaws at dinner in
"common or triple time, according to
"the inftruments that accompany our
"meals.——By dealing the cards at qua-
"drille, how eafy it is to judge if the
"party has an ear!——yonder gentleman
"who comes towards our window, fee how
"he fwings his arms in exact time, true as
"the pendulum of a clock. I can affure
"you, fir, he is great on the violoncello.
"My dear wife fays, the conjugal endear-
"ments are doubly improved, if a hufband
"is a good timeift. She approves of
"triple time; and on this account I for-
"merly had a fervant who play'd in our
"bed-room every Sunday night, 'till we
"flept. And fince I became one of the
"*caftrati*, I have acquired the habit of
"making water at intervals in the trueft
"time like a pig; and may fay, I be-
"lieve, that for exactnefs of ear, I am not
"exceeded by any modern mufician."

This great man then took up a Jew's
harp that lay by him, and with a *twing,*
twang,

twang, twong, moving his finger across his lips, and making faces in the most exact time, he fetched out such prurient harmony, as ravished my very soul, and threw sweet Miss *Ferni* into the most agreeable convulsions.

During our dinner, two of the Doctor's servants entertained us with many excellent and solemn pieces of music. Indeed, I was so solicitous to cut and eat my meat in true time, as I thought my character depended on this circumstance, that I unfortunately cut my lips, and should certainly have fainted at the sight of my own blood, had I not been roused by a warlike symphony on the bag-pipe. Sweet Miss *Ferni* too gave so earnest an attention to the fiddlers, that on their suddenly changing the tune from *Lumps of Pudding*, to *O the Roast Beef of old England*, she swallowed the ivory spoon out of a mustard pot; which, as it stuck across her throat, I am sure must have given that excellent young lady exquisite pain.

pain. Yet did she cough, and even vomit repeatedly in most accurate time, and screamed from fear most harmoniously through the whole gamut, from *a* to *g* inclusively, long after the spoon was restored to its place.

SHEFFIELD.

Dr. *Dilettanti* was so kind as to make me a present of a place in the stage coach to *Sheffield* in my intended journey to *York*, that I might inquire into the present state of the music of that city, and cathedral. Amongst the other passengers, was a gentleman of a grave aspect; who, from his not attending to me at the inn, when I play'd a most inchanting solo on my hautboy, appear'd at first to have no ears, but on further conversation I found him a most agreeable companion. He cry'd up the ingenuity of the *Sheffield* manufacturers, and told me of a new musical instrument, more complicate, he thought, and louder than an organ. The next day he was so good as to accompany me to hear this new organic instrument. The first thing I could observe was a number of iron pipes, and a water wheel to work the large bellows, like that organ of which there is a print in *Kempler's Musurgia*. When the wheel was in motion, I observed many of the notes higher than in any organ I had ever heard; and was told, that these ingenious people had found the only way to produce these was, by boring gun-barrels: to these a symphony was added by files which cut the teeth of large saws, and the mellow tones of two great hammers, which at intervals struck on large pieces of red-hot iron, made a more tremendous and affecting concert, than all the mingled whistles of *Cecilia*'s organ.

I paid a shilling to the performers of this stupendous piece of harmony, at which my grave companion seem'd much delighted, and listen'd to my remarks upon

upon it with the greatest avidity and approbation; " Signor *Collioni*," says he, " your observations inchant me; the most " antient music, as you well explain, was " made by hammers beating upon anvils, " as invented by *Tubal Cain*, and prac- " tised in the shop of his successor, *Vul-* " *can*, tho' *Saturn* is thought to have " been the first of the *castrati*.—But this " invention was not compleat, Signor " *Collioni*, it was not compleat, till this " excellent treble made by boring guns, " and cutting saws was added.—It is now " become the true celebrated, long-lost, " and long-deplored chromatic of the " antients."

" Doubtless you are right in your con- " jectures, reply'd I, Mr. *Hummings*, " (for that was my kind companion's " name) it was music like this, which " could disenchant the moon, and make " trees and stones dance *allemands*. " Would you believe it, Mr. *Hummings*, " I myself once cured a girl bit with a
" tarantula

"tarantula with this simple baffoon?—*Trut,*
"*turrut, phub, phub, bufh!*—This was
"the air, Mr. *Hummings,* you fhall hear
"it—*trut, turrut, phub, phub, bufh:*—
"the girl rifing from her melancholy at-
"titude, danced till the fweat ran down
"to the hem of her fcarlet petticoat;
"and after I had prefented her with a
"bit of money, became fo lively as to
"ftrip herfelf like King *David,* and dance
"like a *Heinel.* I can affure you, Mr.
"*Hummings,* I drove away the evil fpirit,
"and cured her of her tarantulifm that
"night.

"Not unlike this, is a fact recorded
"by the divine *Homer. Ulyffes* had a
"large rent made in his thigh by a wild
"boar,—a terrible animal, Mr. *Hum-*
"*mings:*—well, and what happen'd?—
"why, he only fent for the town-waits,
"and after the firft bar or two had been
"play'd, the blood ftopp'd; and as the
"fiddles proceeded, the wound con-
"tracted, and by the time they had
"finifhed

"finished *Alley Croaker, Moggy Lauder*
"and *A lovely Lass to a Fryar came*, (which
"are all antient *Greek* tunes, sir,) the
"wound was quite healed, and the
"cicatrix as smooth as the back of my
"hand."

During this conversation, an unfortunate accident had happened near us. One of the performers on the hammer and iron had broken his leg by a fall. A surgeon was sent for with all dispatch, but Mr. *Hummings* advised me to try the effect of the bassoon upon him; and, pointing to me, told the people that they need seek no farther, for I was superior to any surgeon. Upon this, untying my green bag, the man cry'd out; he begg'd no instruments might be used. "No, (says "I,) none but a musical instrument." So I began with a gentle blast, and played and sung alternately,—"*You'll ne'er go* "*the sooner to the Stygian Ferry. Let not* "*your noble spirits be cast down, but drink,* "*drink, drink, and be merry.*"—" Give
" me

"me some ale, (cries the wounded man) "I like this Doctor." Afterward I blew till I nearly had burst my cheeks, and then sung, *If 'tis joy to wound a lover*; but the bone would not knit :—indeed I could not make it knit at all—and I don't believe, as Mr. *Hummings* said, that if Dr. *Burney* himself, and all the musicians of Britain, fiddlers, violoncellos, double violoncellos, trumpets, and trumpet-marinos, together with every *Maestro di Capella* in *Italy* had been present, they could have made this bone knit—which, I suppose, was owing to the scorbutic habit of body of the patient; indeed, Mr. *Hummings* attributed it entirely to this cause; for the blood stopped before I had finished the first song.

Nothing worthy remark occur'd in my journey from hence to

YORK,

But at my approach to this celebrated city, my heart leapt for joy as soon as I beheld

beheld the towers of the cathedral; here, says I, I shall be much careffed and followed, I dare believe, as there are so many of the *Dilettanti* who reside within the precincts of this antient seat of music and superstition. This letter, says I, is of ineftimable value, taking it from my pocket, and reading the direction, " For " that incomparable Musician and Anti- " quarian, Dr. *Hiccup*;" doubtless he will pay great attention to his friends at *Lincoln*, who have honoured me with it. The footman shewed me into an elegant parlour, where there was a clock with chimes, so contrived that St. *Peter*, St. *Paul*, and the *Virgin Mary* were seen striking alternately on the bells, and by a sweet trio announced every hour of the day. Dr. *Hiccup* was, it seems, at his devotions, which he always performed in imitation of that great and devout musician, King *David*. He was a tall, bony figure, with a swarthy complexion, and blear eyes. As I sat down he took no notice of me, but continued dancing with a harp in his hand, without his breeches, and with his night-gown and shirt tucked up above his waist; and as he turned himself this way and that, in the gyrations of the dance, all the women and children that were looking in through the window of his parlour, giggled, and made faces, and shewed variety of indecent gesticulations and noises. None of these circumstances, however, interrupted the devotions of this great man.

Never were such charming tunes elicited from mortal harp, *Cambrian* or *Eolic!* the dance was devotion itself in human form! After a little refreshment, this illustrious Musician condescended to entertain me with several interesting particulars of the manner of his life, which I begg'd leave to copy in my pocket book in his presence.

He rose every morning, when his chime-clock struck eleven, (for, like the famous *Chevalier Gluck*, he is too great a genius

genius to rife early) and generally gaped all the time his lady was putting on his breeches. For breakfaſt he always eat rolls and butter, whether in ſummer or winter; and after his breakfaſt paid a ſhort viſit to *Cloacina*, but aſſured me he never uſed old muſic books on this occaſion, even in the moſt urgent neceſſity. He retired to reſt about ten, and ſeldom fail'd once in a month to compliment his lady for undreſſing him.

He communicated many other particulars to me of leſs moment, and was ſo obliging at length to beg I would treat him with an air or two on the baſſoon.

I thought this a good opportunity to give him a ſpecimen of my poetic talents, as well as of my muſical ones, and performed the following ſong, which I compoſed at *Gotham* ſeveral years ago.

"Some came in a waggon, and ſome in a cart;
And many there were that did nothing but ——:
Sing O rare *Nottingham*, *Nottingham* town!
Nottingham town; O rare *Nottingham* town!"

The sweetness of the notes on my bassoon, an instrument whose tone is so like the sound it was to represent, ravished his ears, which he hung quite down on each shoulder, during the whole time of my performance.

I slept this night at Dr. *Hiccup*'s house, and borrowed a shirt and pair of stockings of him. At breakfast I took an opportunity to tell him of the narrowness of my circumstances; but he was suddenly seized by a rapturous fit of devotion, and pulling up his night-gown to his waist, began to sing, and dance, and caper, and kick, to such a degree, that no one in the room was safe: I ran towards the door to save my shins, and the Doctor rising with both feet in the air like a Harlequin, gave me such a horse-kick on my rump, singing at the same time the *March in Saul*, that I descended into the street down five steps, head foremost, and cracked my bassoon in twenty places.

Six

Six hours I attended at the door, but was told by a servant out of a window, that the Doctor was still performing his dance of devotion; and for aught I know, that great man may dance till doom's-day, as I never after could get any other answer at his door.

On more mature reflexion, I thought this behaviour very extraordinary in a brother musician, and one to whom I was so well recommended; but I consoled myself with considering, that though my bassoon was broken in sundry places, yet I had retained the Doctor's shirt and stockings; and that it was very likely my great prototype, Doctor *Burney* himself, had frequently met with the same treatment, tho' his modesty had inclined him to conceal it.

I was now necessitated to travel on foot, and got that evening as far as

BEVERLEY.

Hearing the sound of musical instruments as I passed under a window upon my

my entrance into this town, I enquired at the door if there was a concert performing there, and being anfwered in the affirmative, I immediately produced my bafs viol, and defired to be admitted into the orcheftra as a Dilettante performer. My requeft was readily granted, and I was feated with great refpect next to a gentleman of the profeffion in laced clothes and ruffles. Being indifferently dreffed myfelf, I was refolved to make amends for the inelegance of my figure, by the brilliancy of my performance; but no fooner had I begun to move my bow, than I found the notes of my inftrument perfectly overpowered by the fonorous fnoring of three gentlemen behind me, whom I therefore took the liberty to jog, intreating them for the fake of the whole company, either to keep awake, or fnore in tune. They took this hint in good part. "Thank you kindly, Mafter Fid-
"dler," faid one of them; yawning and ftretching, "I loves mufic mightily, but
"it

" it always puts me to sleep, like a ser-
" mon—Egod I sleep while the organ's
" playing at *Paul*'s." His next neighbour said, he hated profane organs, but
had no objection to fiddles, nor any other
music, except drums, and Scotch tunes.
I wondered much at this latter exception,
as I knew that most people of taste admired Scotch music; but I afterwards
found this antipathy was founded on political sentiments. The other gentleman
added, that for his part, he liked any
music, so as he did not pay the piper;
at which they all laughed. I asked them
if they were *Dilettanti*, to which one of
them answered, " No, nor macaronies;
" nor soup-meagres neither; we are al-
" dermen of London, Sir; Supporters of
" the Bill of Rights, and parliament-
" men, (two of us however, brother
" *Brazen* and I,")—" Ay, ay, cried Mr.
" *Brazen*, and more than that, we are
" all colonels of the Artillery Company,
" governors of *Bartholomew* and *Blue-*
" *coat*

" coat hospitals, *Antigallicans, Wilko-*
" *nians, Albions, Old Souls, Lumber-*
" *troopers,* and *Knights of the Brush*."—
Though I had never heard of any of these dignities before, yet as I have an innate veneration for titles of all sorts, I made as profound and respectful a bow to these noble strangers, (grounding my bass viol at the same time,) as Dr. *Burney* could have done to any of the Electors of Germany. Indeed I was much prepossessed in favour of their rank and quality, by the broad lace they wore on their scarlet waistcoats, and the gold chain which encircled the neck of one of them. I made no doubt therefore of their veracity, when they assured me that the titles they had enumerated were more honourable than any his majesty could bestow. They seemed much pleased with the respect I shewed them, and having their pockets stuffed with melons and pine-apples, desired me to eat some, which at first I declined, fearing to rob them of such

such excellent fruit; but Mr. *Brazen* pressing me to accept it, and assuring me, I could not rob *them*, for it cost *them* nothing; I could not withstand so much politeness, and put a melon and a pineapple into my pocket for my supper. The aldermen soon devoured the rest, and then protesting they could not keep awake any longer than they were eating, politely retired to the further corner of the room to refresh themselves with another nap, while I returned to my bass viol, and being that evening in fine spirits, and very enthusiastic, acquired great applause and received many thanks for my performance.

Early the next morning I set forward in my way to *Durham*, whither I was necessitated to travel on foot; and by playing the *Black Joke*, *Murdoch O'Blaney*, and other sentimental tunes to the girls of the villages I pass'd through, procured food and lodging, which my brother of the String had refused me.

DARLINGTON.

Here I waited on the *Maestro di Capella*, or clerk of the parish, who I may assert has the finest nasality, or nose-intonation, that ever was given to a Psalm tune, and the thorough base of his *Amen*, was quite astonishing.

I had got some wax'd thread at the cobler's, and mended my basloon, which was so well received at this church, that the 'Squire's lady invited me to Dinner. " Good Signior *Collioni*, says she, you
" have charmed, you have enraptured
" me; pray, has the wind which escapes
" out at the end of your instrument any
" smell?"———" smell! says I, no, madam,
" not unless I eat onions." At this all the ladies laughed most extravagantly.

However, the 'Squire after dinner gave me a recommendatory letter to great Mr. *Eccho* of *Durham*, principal performer belonging to that opulent cathedral; and withal told me, that Mr. *Eccho* had so

long

long apply'd himself to musical notes, that he had utterly forgot all articulate language. That he preached, conversed, prayed, scolded, swore, and talk'd bawdy, all on the fiddle, without uttering a word, or even making a sign with his fingers.—

DURHAM,

At my introduction to Mr. *Eccho*, I began a long complimental speech, which I had been some time studying.—" Most " respectable sir, whose soul is a soul of " harmony, and whose body is like a base- " viol."—Here he snatch'd up his fiddle with an air of great complacency, and drawing the bow gently over the strings said, as plain as if he had spoke it, " O, sir, " your most obedient; you compliment " me indeed, sir, too much." I then told him how long a journey I had performed on foot, and that the dusty roads had made me dry. He snatched up his violin, and before he had play'd above a

bar

bar or two, in came a footman with a jug of delicate ale. Next I mentioned modeſtly my having eat nothing all day.— " Truť, trut, biſh, baſh, buſh," cries the fiddle—" Indeed, ſir, replies I, I don't " faſt for the ſake of devotion"—" ir, " er, ar, querr, quorr, quurr"—quoth the fiddle, and in came a ſurloin of cold beef, and muſtard and bread, in the twinkling of a fiddle-ſtick.

" This, gentlemen," quoth I, " is
" greater than *Orpheus* and *Eurydice*, or
" the *Serpent* ;—no, no, *Orpheus* could
" do no ſuch things as theſe—ale and
" beef were a note or two above his
" fiddle!"

Soon after came in Mr. *Eccho*'s wife, with a " what the deuce are you about, " bringing beggars into my houſe ?"—Mr. *Eccho* catched up the fiddle, and ſuch a jar did I never hear—" *arg, erg, urg, gir,* " *gor, gur*"—I warrant you madam be- came as dumb as if ſhe were inchanted.

Indeed,

Indeed, hearing this lady give me the opprobrious name of beggar, I took care to shew the diamond ring on my little finger, which I always wear when I perform in public, which might give her a better opinion of me, 'tho' indeed it is only a Bristol stone, and that I pay a silver-smith two pence a week for the use of; I would at the same time have hired a laced waistcoat, but was asked a shilling a week, tho' I am sure the lace had been twice turn'd; yet, if I had hired it, I dare say Dr. *Hiccup* would scarcely have kicked me out of his house.

CARLISLE.

At *Carlisle* I waited on Lord *Diddledoodle* with proper musical credentials: he was seated opposite to a glass practising some *solfeggi* on the flute, and attending to the gracefulness of his own attitude. " Most illustrious Peer, says I," (making a bow to the very ground) " your noble " ancestors gain'd victory in the hardy
" fields

"fields of war, but you by music civilize and harmonize mankind; with what rapture must they lean from their starry mansions to hear and see your immortal powers of harmony and grace!" I stopp'd, and on looking up, found that his lordship had not attended to a word I had spoken, nor seemed conscious of my being in the room;---but as great geniuses are often absent, I repeated my compliment in a louder voice, and approaching, was amazed to find that his lordship was quite deaf, deaf as a post; and yet he executed the most difficult passages in music with the greatest grace and manner,—better, I dare say, than if he had heard his own performance.

When his lordship had perceived me, he approached me with the utmost politeness, and made signs for me to sit down, and accompany him upon the bassoon, which I did 'till dinner-time. After dinner, I intreated my lady *Diddle-doodle* to prevail upon the noble lord to sing, which he he did; but I was rather difappointed at finding that his voice was only packthread *. However, "he fung in tune; "had a fhake, and was far from vulgar." My lady afterwards made ample amends by her own finging. Her voice was a fkane of filk, without the leaft mixture of worfted. She underftood all the lights and fhades of melody. Her back-ground; her mezzotints; and her clare-obfcure were charming, "and there was fuch a "roundnefs and dignity in all the tones, "that every thing fhe did became in- "terefting."

It was in this part of *England*, I paid a vifit to Mr. *Quaver*, with recommendatory letters from lord *Diddle-doodle*; I found him to be a gentleman of confiderable and original mufical genius; his tafte was pure, chafte, refined; and his execution, particularly upon the Jew's harp, was exquifite; he executed with great

---

* "His voice is now but a thread."
TOUR THRO' ITALY.

tafte

taste and powers, *Nancy Dawson*, *Lillabullero*, and *Old Sir Simon the king*. After dinner he explained to me his system for the improvement of sound, which was at once sublime and original. " The Author " of Nature," said he, " has with an equal " and judicious hand distributed his gifts " among his creatures: to one he has given " strength; to another, dexterity; to a " third, perseverance; in the same man- " ner has he divided the agreeable quali- " fications; and the courtier and the fine " gentleman need not blush to receive in- " struction from the spaniel and the " monkey---Now as the philosopher mo- " dels his life upon an imitation of the " virtues of animals, the true connoisseur " will do the same"---there he stopp'd, as if afraid to explain himself; but I told him, that there was something so original and masterly in his conceptions that I should never be easy, until he communicated them. Upon which, after a short pause, he seized me by the hand, and

grasping

grasping it with affection, " since, said
" he, I find in you the true spirit of your
" science, I will no longer maintain any
" reserve. Know then, that after a pro-
" found meditation upon the sublimest
" mysteries of our profession, I have traced
" them up to the creation"—" how! said
" I, with amaze, I thought that the greatest
" Antiquarians had never brought them
" with any certainty higher than the De-
" luge." I knew," said he, " I should sur-
" prize you; but it is certain that *Adam*,
" among his other qualifications, possessed
" that of expressing every sound that ever
" has or can be uttered; hence he could
" not only sing bass and treble, counter-
" tenor, and soprano to admiration; but
" also squeak like a pig, croak like a frog,
" bellow like a bull, whinny like a colt,
" and bray like an ass.

" It is true, that the greater part of these
" faculties was taken from him at the
" Fall, and the rest have been very spa-
" ringly bestowed upon his descendants;

" from

"from hence arises that degeneracy into which music has fallen in the modern ages of the world: that sublime science, instead of expressing the natural passions, by a judicious imitation of the tones of beasts; instead of roaring out the lion's rage; bellowing the jealousy of the bull, or chanting the amorous passions of the nightingale, is become a meer unmeaning jargon, without force or energy, and its professors and admirers are dwindled into the most contemptible part of the creation; quavering eunuchs, unfeeling prostitutes, insignificant blockheads, wretches without head, or heart, or sentiment, or enthusiasm."—I was sensible that there was much truth in this gentleman's observations, though I could not assent to every thing he said against our modern *virtuosi*, among whom envy itself must acknowledge there are some accomplished characters; and the eighteenth century will always glory in having produced a

KING

KING of PRUSSIA, an ELECTOR of MUNICH, a TENDUCCI, and a BURNEY.

"But," said my friend, "perceiving
"this to be the lamentable ftate of things,
"I have with true and indefatigable in-
"duftry applied myfelf to the reftoration
"of the firft *Adamitical* harmony; I have
"felected the moft admirable notes from
"every animal, and have already acquired
"a tolerable proficiency in bellowing,
"braying and grunting: I indeed found
"that the *fquall* of the peacock was two
"notes too high for my voice; but in re-
"turn, if I may fay fo without vanity, I
"can infpire every hen and gofling in the
"yard with tender fentiments. I have,
"befides this, collected every great natu-
"ral genius that I have found among the
"brute creation; I have a young he-afs
"who has an admirable bafs; a young
"hog, (a *caftrato*) who fings a counter-
"tenor; and a dear little cat, whom, in
"honour of that illuftrious name, fo ce-
"lebrated in the Doctor's tour, I call

"MIN-

" MINGOTTI, who has an excellent tre-
" ble, and a surprising *portamento.* But
" why waste I time in description? you
" shall see my scholars, and my *schola.*"

Saying this, he led me to a large building, which resembled a barn, where we were received by the *Maestro di Capella,* who was an old and deaf huntsman. The first object I beheld was a beautiful she-ass in a *Mecklinburgh* night-cap, who brayed a solo. Her voice was one of the clearest, sweetest, truest, most powerful and extensive I ever heard. " In com-
" pass, it is from Bb on the fifth space
" in the bass, to D in *alt,* full steady and
" equal; her shake was good, and her
" *portamento* admirably free from the
" nose, mouth, or throat." We were then entertained by a duet between the *Mingotti,* and a large raven, in the *chromatic,* which grew more spirited by my friend's pulling a bone out of his pocket, which he threw to the performers, and thereby produced a *conflicta.* I then told my

my friend that I would willingly hear the *caſtrato*, but he answered he was afraid the *Caffarelli* could not oblige me in that particular, as he had unfortunately taken cold by rolling too long upon an unaired dunghill, and was then actually in a courſe of ſugar-candy. However, he threw a turnip to encourage him to exert himſelf; and I could judge from what I then heard, that he is likely to become a moſt maſterly performer.

My friend then tied ſtrings to the ears of ſix young greyhound puppies, which he twitch'd with ſo much art and judgment by means of a pully, that I think the effect was equal to any *viol di gamba* I ever heard, not excepting that of the Elector of *Munich*.

He then ſuſpended two cats by the tails, which he contrived ſhould alternately bob upon the noſes of two ſucking pigs, who were tied by the hind-legs to the floor: though I obſerved theſe performers were ſomewhat embarraſſed in

their

their manner, yet I could not but acknowledge the effect was quite original and truly theatric.

Mr. *Quaver* then told me that he had formerly introduced some of these performers to sing at a concert, but without success: and he made great complaints of the unpoliteness of the audience, which he said could sit with patience three hours to listen to the unmeaning trills of heroes in hoop-petticoats, and *Italian* vagabonds in a strange language, while they would not bestow one half hour upon the voice of nature and their brethren *. Tho' I was quite ignorant of the facts he alluded to, yet, like Dr. BURNEY, I was so partial to talents, wherever I found them, that I could not help condoling with my kind host upon the occasion; and after

---

* " Guadagni complains of illiberal treatment from the public, who, when he sung in the Opera of *Orfeo*, merely to oblige them and Sir W. W. without fee or reward, hissed him for going off the stage when he was encored, with no other design than *to return in character*."
TOUR THRO' GERMANY.

having

having bemoaned the degeneracy of the times, and wished him succefs in his truly original undertaking, which I promifed him I would take due notice of in my intended work, I fet forward on my journey toward *Lancafter*.

That day I met with no mufical incident, but the next, as I walked along the high road, I thought I heard a tinkling of bells, not fo loud as thofe of horfes in a team, but much more harmonious. I took the liberty therefore of following my ears, and fcrambling over a clipp'd hedge found myfelf upon a fine lawn belonging to a gentleman's feat, and foon perceived that this mufic proceeded from *tintinnabula* bells faftened on the necks of a flock of fheep grazing near me. Tho' I know Dr. Burney treats all *Carillons* with fovereign contempt, I confefs I was much pleafed with thefe, and taking out my tablets, followed them, and pricked down the tunes they played, which indeed were full of pretty things. The fheep too accompanied

companied them like "performers who "had seen some service," except one ram, who, tho' a veteran in years, bleated the thorough-bass as much out of tune as if he had just 'listed. As I observed however that he neither wanted compass nor taste, I ran up to him, and catching hold of his horns, bleated the true time into his ears, which he endeavoured to imitate with all his might, and I make no doubt that I should soon have remedied the only defect I found in this pastoral band, but lo! while I was thus engaged, a rude fellow in a fustian frock and laced hat, coming behind me, seized me by the collar, and almost throttled me, roaring out at the same time, "O you gal"lows sheep-stealing thief, have I caught "you in the fact at last?" and without allowing me breath to answer, dragged me to an alcove at a little distance, where sat a young gentleman in a fantastic Arcadian habit, playing upon a guittar; who at our entrance reproved the servant

for

for interrupting him before he had finished his folo. " A fiddle-stick for *folo*,"
said the fellow, " this is no time to be
" strumming of cat-gut, pray come and
" assist me to take this sheep-stealer be-
" fore your father and get his *mittimus*
" signed." Indeed, replied the other, I
will not be disturbed by such trifles; and
immediately began singing, with infinite
fire and expression,

" *Ye shepherds give ear to my lay,*
" *And take no more heed of my sheep.*"
I was so struck with his masterly performance, that not being able to clap my
hands together, in token of applause, I
cried out, *bravissimo! encora!* " Ay, said
the servant, " the dog calls for the rest
" of the gang—we shall be murdered in
" sight of our own house."—I protested
I was no sheep-stealer, but a musician on
his travels, which the young gentleman
said he believed, as I seemed to have a
very good ear, and added,

" The man that has *no* music in his soul,

"And is *not* touch'd by concord of sweet sounds,
"*He*'s fit for treasons, stratagems, and spoils."

To which the fellow answered, that a man might be a sheep-stealer and a musicianer too, and swore it was a fiddler at a wake that robbed all the neighbour's hen-roosts; I submitted to go before the justice quietly, and the young Arcadian followed, singing and playing as he walked along in the most pathetic manner,

My sheep I've forsaken, and left my sheep-hook,
And all the gay haunts of my youth I've forsook.

When we came before the old gentleman, the man made his charge, which I answered by telling the story as I have just related it; the young gentleman made an eloquent speech in my defence, and concluded with singing most divinely,

O clear him then from this offence,
Thy love, his duty prove, &c.

The servant desired I might be searched, assuring the justice that he had felt a blunderbuss under my coat, and that I had papers about me, which might dis-

cover

cover my accomplices. Upon the search, my bassoon, the only weapon I had, was produced, to the utter confusion of my unrelenting prosecutor; and my MSS. being handed up, the justice read aloud the title in these words, "An Enquiry "into the present state of the Music of "the Spheres, with the Overture to the "last Eclipse of the Moon, and a disser- "tation on the celestial fiddle-stick, vul- "garly called the rain-bow." As soon as he had read this, the justice jumped up, and walked away; declaring I was just such a poor crack-brain'd fellow as his son, and that we were fit company for each other. As soon as he had quitted the bench, the young gentleman came up to me, and apologizing for his father's rude behaviour, requested I would pass an hour with him in his study. This invitation I readily accepted, notwithstanding the character I had just heard of him, for I am of opinion, that a little perturbation of the faculties is not amiss, and indeed is unavoidable in a young musician of fire and imagination. I found he had written several pieces relative to the improvement of musical science; tho' his modesty had prevented their publication. Among other manuscripts which he shewed me, was a proposal for carrying on war without bloodshed, in which, his scheme was to arm the soldiers with musical instruments and fire-arms; which latter should be only discharged into the air at proper intervals, for the sake of musical explosions; and that the bass should be played by great cannon, in the same harmless manner, so that each army should form a complete band, and the battle should be lost by that general which should first play out of tune. I much applauded this scheme, as well on account of the grand effect which musical cannon must produce, as for the sake of all the Christian blood which would be saved by the adoption of this mode of decision among the powers of Europe;

for

for, like the Dr. " tho' I love mufic very
" well, I love humanity ftill better," in
which particular we differ much from
that great flutift and warrior the king of
Pruffia. He next fhewed me a plan of a
work he was then upon, which was
turning Mr. Garrick's celebrated *Ode on
Shakefpeare* into an Italian Opera, a fpe-
cies of writing, which, he faid, it much
refembled in ftile, imagery, poetry and
fentiment. " Mark," fays he, " the pictu-
" refque beauty of thefe two lines, which
" are the laft I have tranflated :
   " *The little loves, like bees,*
   " *Cluft'ring, and climbing up his knees.*"
" What an amazing effect this perfonifica-
" tion of the loves will have on the ftage,
" when the audience behold Signor *Rauzini*
" in the character of Shakefpeare, with a
" hive of Mr. *Wildman*'s bees climbing up
" his legs, with the queen-bee at their
" head, in the character of Venus, who
" will be taught to perform a moft en-
" chanting folo *hum!* After fhe has faluted
" the

"the poet, he, she, and her subject bees,
"all smile; for, as the inimitable Mr.
"*Garrick* expresses it,

"*They* SMILE *while they're giving,*
"*He* SMILES *at receiving,*
"*A treasure of joy.*"

After I had sufficiently complimented him upon this work, and told him that I thought the Ode would be wonderfully improved in his hands, we discoursed upon the subject of Dr. Burney's travels, of which he was a professed admirer; and mentioned with great approbation that "curious operation" which the Dr. was informed, was "performed fre-
"quently at Naples, of cutting the glands
"of the throat, when so inflated, or big,
"as to obstruct the free passage of the
"voice." This anecdote had given my friend a hint of greater improvements; "We are too sparing," says he, "of the
"knife—and when we are arrived at
"castration, think the voice is as perfect
"as art can make it, but we stop short
"of

" of perfection. There are other super-
" fluities besides the *testes* and glands of
" the throat which obstruct the free
" course of the voice. Believe me, Sir,
" the TONGUE itself might well be spared,
" which only serves to articulate sounds
" in speaking, but is an incumbrance to
" a fine singer. Do me the favour, Sir,
" to sing one air with this ivory bit in
" your mouth, to keep down your tongue,
" and you will be surprized at the dif-
" ference it makes in the mellowness of
" the tone, and the roundness of the
" volume of voice." Saying this, he
fetched an ivory instrument out of his
drawer, which he fixt in my mouth, and
fastened to my head, like a horse's bit.
He then continued his discourse thus:
" There is in fact no difference betwixt
" vocal and instrumental music: for as
" the soul is rightly defined by an antient
" philosopher to be harmony, so is the
" body a natural musical instrument; of
" which the lungs form the bellows, and
"the

"the wind-pipe a paſſage for the air, as
"in an organ; the uſe of this bit is to
"preſerve the volume of voice entire, by
"preſſing down the tongue; and, by the
"bye, if the teeth were pulled out too,
"it would leave the paſſage infinitely
"freer from obſtruction."—Here I endeavoured to interrupt him, for I found the bit very painful, but not being able to articulate, he thought I was attempting to ſing, and cried out, "Stay a mo-
"ment, my dear friend, let me juſt put
"two plugs into your noſtrils to prevent
"the air from iſſuing out at thoſe aper-
"tures." I was reſolved not to endure this, and looked round for the door, in order to ſecure a retreat, while he thus went on:—" I always wear plugs when
"I ſing, but I have a great notion that
"if holes were bored at proper diſtances
"along the ſide of the noſe, it would
"make no bad flute. Now, Sir, give
"me leave to ſhew you how much far-
"ther the jaws ought to be diſtended by
"the

"the lancet, and where the glands should
"be cut."—Saying this, he drew a penknife out of his side-pocket; but as I had all this time been sidling toward the door, (being now fully convinced he was rather more disturbed in his faculties than a good theorist ought to be,) out I flew, and never once looked behind me till I was fairly out of sight of the house; when at my leisure I untied my jaws which now began to ach confoundedly, and walked on very well pleased to find that I had not left my tongue behind me, and reflected upon the truth of the poet's observation,

> Great wit to madness nearly is allied,
> And thin partitions do the bounds divide.

I passed through the towns of *Lancaster* and *Preston* without any adventure, and the next day arrived at

LIVERPOOL.

Here I instantly went to pay my respects to Mr. *Cable*, who had formerly com-

commanded a ship in the African slave-trade, but had long quitted that inhuman employment, and given himself up entirely to the cultivation of music. I found him sitting in a pleasant summer-house, which he had erected on the top of a decayed elm, and with infinite taste fitted up in imitation of a ship's cabbin. Here he was solacing himself with a pipe and a bowl of grog. He very civilly invited me to sit down, and when I had presented my recommendatory letter to him, he put it into his pocket, and said, he would overhaul it at his leisure, though I afterward found that the captain had never had the advantage of learning to read or write. After having emptied two bowls in the most amicable manner, the captain very civilly proposed to me to sing, which I instantly complied with, and began tuning up, *Let not age thy bloom ensnare, &c.* but was much surprized to hear him roar out, before I had finished the first line, that " d—— his
" eyes,

"eyes, he did not like that palaver, but "wanted to hear *Hearts of Oak*, or something that was jolly." I very submissively excused myself as never having learnt that air, and he, accepting my apology, told me, as I could not sing, I might have a bout with my fiddle, as he supposed I knew how to scrape that. Though this behaviour was very opposite to that softness which the love of music generally inspires, and made me envy the good fortune of my great master, who in his travels had always performed to princes, and electors; yet not chusing to exasperate my host, who was a middle-sized, broad-shouldered man, with bow-legs, and a fist like a shoulder of mutton, I took up my violoncello, and began an overture which I thought capable of disarming the greatest ruggedness of temper. Full twenty minutes I continued playing without interruption, congratulating myself upon the conquest I had gained over the captain's ferocity, and reflecting with

admiration upon the amazing powers of sound, which could thus silence the jarring passions, and soften the roughest dispositions. "O why," said I to myself, "is not the great Dr. here, to share in the triumphs of his pupil?" Saying this, I ventured to steal a glance at a pierglass, that was opposite to me, in order to adjust my attitude, when, with the utmost surprize and indignation, I beheld the captain, whom I thought enraptured by my skill, fast asleep, and nodding in his elbow chair. I confess, I was scarcely able to contain my fury at this affront, but thinking it inconsistent with my character to express my feelings in any other than a musical way; I sang with great vehemence—*I rage—I burn—despair—despair.——To arms, to arms, your silver trumpets sound*—and touching my violoncello in the rudest manner, I awoke such sounds of horror and anguish; I made the strings so responsive to the agitations of my mind, that the captain started up
pre-

precipitately from his seat, overset the bowl of liquor, and blasting my eyes, asked me what I meant by making such a catterwauling? There was something so terrific in his looks and gestures, that I could not resist the impulse I experienced, to pacify him by my apologies. These he kindly received, and we cemented our reconciliation by another bowl of grog; after which the captain felt himself in such good humour, that he insisted upon my giving him my impartial opinion upon his own musical acquirements, and ringing the bell, ordered his *Gom-gom* to be brought in. This instrument was a wooden bow, the ends of which were confined by a dried, and hollow gut, into which the captain blew, scraping upon it at the same time with an old fiddle-stick, stamping upon the ground, and roaring out, Ho! ho! with such a force of lungs, and extension of voice, that at length, unable to bear the horrid discord any longer, I begged him to desist.

defift. He then told me that he had acquired the knowledge of this inftrument during the courfe of feveral voyages to the coaft of Africa, and that his proficiency was allowed to be fo great, that the king of *Benin* had offered to make him his prime minifter, provided he would have continued at his court, and that he had fecretly received propofals of marriage from a princefs of *Monomatapa*. " But," added he, " I loved old England fo well
" that I did not chufe to ftay with their
" black majefties, and having made a
" very pretty fortune, retired hither,
" where I live very happily, and amufe
" myfelf every afternoon with my fa-
" vourite inftrument."—He then afked me with a very felf-fufficient fmile, or rather grin, if I did not prefer it to an overgrown fiddle, and all the Italian whimfies, and tweedle-dums, that people played upon in thefe days?—I thought myfelf and my profeffion fo much infulted by this impertinent difcourfe, that I could

not

not help telling him with a contemptuous smile, that the music was adapted to the musician, that it might do very well for seafaring people, but that to cultivated ears it was absolutely barbarous; and therefore I advised him to confine his exhibitions to his negro princes and princesses, and never again attempt to perform before any person possessed of the least brilliancy of finger. Saying this, I took up my violoncello, that by the execution of a most masterly *capricio*, I might convince him of his ignorance, and my own skill. But scarce had I touched the chords before this unmannerly tarpaulin burst into the most reproachful language. He called me a lousy rascal; a squeaking son of a b——h; a lubberly gut-scraper; and not contented with this contumelious treatment, when I attempted to vindicate my character, he knocked me down at one blow, and after this unprecedented outrage, ordered two black slaves to bring him a rope, and swore he would keelhaul

haul me. In vain did I remonstrate against this inhuman treatment, in sounds which might have " melted rocks, and softened " things inanimate to pity;" I was dragged to a large horse-pond, in the middle of which was a kind of Indian canoe, under which I was three times successively drawn by two ropes, while the captain stood on the bank, shaking his sides with laughter, and playing a warlike measure with his *gom-gom*. Having undergone this savage operation, I was thrust headlong into the street, my teeth chattering, and my whole body shivering with cold and affright; and the captain muttering out the most barbarous jests on my condition, threw my violoncello after me, and shut the door.

In this distressed situation did I wander about the town, hooted at by the boys, and exciting the derision of the vulgar; till at length a very decent woman, who lives at the sign of the French horn, (to which circumstance I principally ascribe her

her humanity) kindly invited me in, and after drying myself at her fire, and drinking a quartern of gin, to prevent my catching cold, I slept very comfortably that night upon a flock bed, and set out early the next morning for

CHESTER.

The ablution I had received the day before having answered every purpose of clean linen, I ventured with very little alteration in my dress to present myself to Dr. *Smirk*, a dignified clergyman in that city. I found the Doctor so busied in learning a new opera tune, that though I repeatedly bowed, and attempted to speak, he took no manner of notice of me. At length, having exhausted his breath, he threw himself negligently down upon a sopha, and rolling his eyes round the room, beheld me in the corner where I had seated myself. Instantly he rang his bell, and reproving his servant for suffering any more curates to interrupt him in his studies, he ordered him to turn me out of the house. Though I was somewhat daunted at this extraordinary reception, yet I plucked up sufficient courage to inform him, that I was no curate, but a musician errant, whom one of his friends had taken the liberty of recommending to him for his protection, and informing him of the purport of my journey, I added, that I doubted not, under his auspices, *Chester* would prove one of the most interesting articles in my collection. The Doctor seemed much mollified by this compliment, and ordering the man to bring in his flute, he practised several new *solfeggi*, on which he desired my opinion; I told him that I thought " his hand was firm and brilliant, his taste and expression admirable, and his steadiness in time such as a *Dilettante* is seldom possessed of." I begged the favour of hearing him sing, which he readily granted, but before he began, he ordered his servant to bring in his

his *Dilettante* ring and wig. Seeing that he had excited my wonder, he very obligingly explained himself, by telling me, that, as nothing added so much to the power of music as the dress of the performer, and as no part of dress was more striking and important, than that of the head and finger, he had, during his tour to the Continent, provided rings and wigs for every species of music that he could ever be called upon to perform. He shewed me a spruce scratch neatly powdered, with a tyburn-top, and a large ruby in the shape of a bleeding heart, which, he said, he wore when he performed amorous ditties to the ladies; and he assured me that he never ventured to sing before the fair sex, without using Lord *Chesterfield*'s receipt for the teeth, which he recommended upon his own experience, as being one of the most valuable articles in the works of that great man. He had also a large full-flowing tye, (the invention of which, and the adapting it

to his features, he told me, had cost him three years) in which he preached, together with an antique gem curiously adorned with a masterly representation of the god *Priapus*; this last, however, he very rarely used, except when he preached charity-sermons. He also shewed me a very handsome bob, together with a pair of doe-skin breeches, neatly embroidered at the flaps, and a pair of hussar boots laced at the seams, all which, he intended to wear that night at the catch-club, to which he kindly offered to introduce me. In the course of our conversation, he told me, that his preferment had been principally owing to a young lord, with whom he had had the good fortune to make the tour of Europe, as a travelling tutor: that my lord being equally fond of music and horses, usually rode post; while he followed him at his leisure in a chaise, bringing with him his lordship's favourite cremona, together with a large shock dog; which at his
leisure

leisure hours his lordship instructed in the arts of fetching and carrying, and walking upon his hinder legs. He said, that his tenderness for this respectable animal, together with his skill in cooking *macaroni*, and his great powers in singing catches, had recommended him to the acquaintance and patronage of several of the prime nobility.

In the evening I accompanied the Doctor equipped in the habiliments I have described, to the sign of the Yacht, where the weekly meeting of his brother musicians and divines was held. Here I had the pleasure of hearing him join in *Which is the properest day to drink?* and several other witty and sentimental catches, with great taste, humour, and musical powers. A very pretty band constantly attended this assembly; and what surprized me much at the time, was to observe Dr. *Smirk* as soon as he entered the room, go up to the performers, and after making them a genteel bow, pull one of them

them by the nose; give another a box on the ear; and a third a kick on the breech, till he had saluted the whole band in the same rough manner, which uncouth compliment they seemed to take with wonderful christian patience, and submission. This, however, the Doctor afterwards told me was his constant custom; for he said " he was a rigid disciplinarian," and regularly tuned his musicians, as he was pleased to call it, in this manner once a week: " For," added he, " it is a me-
" lancholy reflection to make, that few
" composers are well treated by an or-
" chestra, till they have used the per-
" formers roughly and made themselves
" formidable."

On our return from the concert, I hinted to Dr. *Smirk*, that it was a great pity the world should not enjoy the benefit of the many curious observations he must have made in his continental tour; and though Dr. *Burney* had almost exhausted the subject of music, yet I should think it

no

no disgrace for men of the first talents to glean after that celebrated genius, and that there was a variety of other polite subjects, particularly cookery, amply sufficient to immortalize the labours of any other traveller. The Doctor smiling told me, that he had indeed thrown together a few observations, in the form of a journal, with which, he hinted, he might be induced to oblige the world, as soon as he had a sufficient number of respectable friends to persuade him to their publication. He said, that in the small compass of a few sheets, which a bookseller by the help of a proper type and margin would scarcely be able to dilate into two octavo volumes, he had treated of almost every subject. "For the mathematician," says he, "I have a new theory of comets, "though never having learned arithmetic "myself, it is now under the correction "of the master of the free-school: for "the physician, there are many great "discoveries in electricity, by which I
"prove

"prove that the five senses, and the soul itself, are nothing more than a peculiar kind of electricity; together with some fine observations on *vacuums,* and the cure of diseases by *silk waistcoats:* For the moralists, I have several pretty reflections; particularly that the ideas of right and wrong are not the same in any two places under the sun: and for the ladies, for whom indeed, as being at present the ultimate judges of all philosophical treatises, my whole work is peculiarly calculated; there is my continually recurring description of teadrinking, horse-races, processions, and the game of cross purposes."

After this conversation I retired to rest upon a down-bed, in an elegant apartment. The next day the Doctor having furnished me with letters to several of his acquaintance in different parts of my route, was also so kind as to permit me to ride behind his servant, who was going great part of my way to *Wolverhampton,*

hampton, upon one of his coach-horses, where I arrived after a journey of three days.

WOLVERHAMPTON.

As I entered this town, I was agreeably surprized by hearing a grand chorus of vocal and instrumental music, among which I plainly distinguished the marrow bones and cleavers, and the English horn. I stood still some time to observe the *diminuendo* and *crescendo:* at length the performers and the procession approaching nearer, I discovered it to be the triumphal entry of a new knight of a neighbouring shire. Imagination can conceive nothing more striking and august. First marched four and twenty patriots, without breeches, distinguished by blue cockades, or blue garters, who made the air resound with liberty and independency. After these came a celebrated musician, who regulated the march of the whole band by the cadences of his fiddle: this gentleman's finger was very neat and rapid; but I could not help lamenting that his inſtrument was very much out of tune. After theſe followed fifteen performers upon the marrow-bones and cleavers, all in blue aprons and blue night-caps; and three upon the Britiſh horn, finging the following grand chorus; of which I was informed both the words and muſic had been compoſed by very great men.

> " Then chear up brave lads of our
>   famous town!
> Is it not a fine ſight
> To ſee our good knight
> On his nag bolt upright?——
> He'll maul ye the courtiers,
> And all their ſupporters,
> And fill the whole county with praiſe
>   and renown."

After theſe rode the ſucceſsful candidate himſelf upon a beautiful dappled mule: this

this animal he had exprefly chofen, to exprefs his perfeverance in the track which he had once entered upon, his patience in attending upon public bufinefs; his inflexibility in oppofition; and above all his exceeding love to his country, for whofe dear fake it is fometimes the duty of a member of the Houfe of Commons to defcend within one degree of an afs; and be prepared to go yet greater lengths if neceffary. Behind him came an innumerable train of the principal gentlemen of the town, confifting of button-makers; blackfmiths; coal-heavers; nail-makers; iron-fplitters; knife-grinders; barbers; apothecaries; and taylors; fome of thefe gentlemen rode upon horfes, others upon affes; part carried their wives and children, and part their miftreffes upon the fame horfe: fome had the implements of their trade, fuch as brafs fenders; fyringes; clofe-ftools; and chamber-pots; tied to long poles by blue ribbands, infcribed

scribed with the name of the representative: some were hollowing, others singing, some roaring, and others vomiting: in short, it was altogether the most august spectacle I had ever seen. After gazing some time I felt myself on a sudden inspired with that enthusiasm which elevates the soul above the vulgar restrictions which reason imposes upon unemulative minds, and thinking this a proper occasion to immortalize myself, and signalize my art, I gave a penny to a dustman to let me ascend the lofty altitudes of his cart. As soon as I was there, I touched my violoncello with unusual ardour, singing at the same time an *extempore* song in praise of the candidate, wherein I celebrated after the manner of the ancient bards, his lineage derived from the gods; the immortal actions of his illustrious ancestors, who had cleared this island of wolves and other monsters; I then transided to the gentleman himself,
whom

whom I exalted as a demi-god, or at least an hero: I praised the majesty of his person, and the melody of his voice; which I compared to that of an Arcadian nightingale, bemoaning his mate upon a flowery spray. I then declared that he united in himself the virtues and excellencies of his whole line: that he was a self-taught orator; a patriot; and a politician; I compared his mule to the famous *Bucephalus*, and himself to *Alexander*, making his triumphal entry into *Babylon* after the conquest of a thousand nations. I concluded my elegant panegyric, by congratulating this island upon its numbering so great a character among its legislators; one who would extend its commerce, and its empire; encourage its manufactures, particularly that of buttons; patronize the fine arts; make the banks of the Thames echo with Italian airs; introduce castration among all classes of mankind; and extirpate the whole breed of foxes from the face of the earth.

I am

I am the more particular in this account of my song, because I am willing to transmit to posterity the ungrateful treatment I met with, in return for so sublime a panegyric: a treatment, which I should have escaped amongst the most barbarous nations, since with them the character of a bard, or fiddler, has been always accounted sacred. How much more shocking then must it appear in the inhabitants of a country which has long been the seat of arts and polite manufactures? But, this is not the first time that I have experienced the ingratitude of mankind, nor I fear the last! I comfort myself therefore with reflecting that in former times *Romulus* and *Alfred*, and in the present Signior *Giardini*, and Dr. *Burney*, have met with similar treatment; though the first pair introduced arts and civilization into their respective countries, and the second have attempted a greater action, that of castrating the children of the Foundling Hospital.

But

But I will trespass no longer upon my reader's patience, whose sympathetic breast is I doubt not by this time agitated by a war of passions! Scarce had I arrived at the conclusion of my song, before, instead of the admiration and applause which I had so well deserved, I was saluted with a general hiss; the representative himself, from whom I confess I expected an handsome present, or at least an invitation to dinner, smacked his whip three times, and exclaimed with a terrible oath: "This here man, gentlemen, is a "ministerial tool, and all that he says is "unconstitutional." Scarce had he spoken, before a rotten egg, thrown by an unknown hand, struck me upon the left eye, and besmeared my face with its fetid contents. I attempted to speak, but a second hurled with greater dexterity, entered and filled up the orifice of my mouth; and as I prepared to make a precipitate retreat from the elevated station

tion which I had so unfortunately chosen, a turnip of an unusual size struck me upon the head, and levelled me with the dust. Three times did I attempt to rise, and as often was I knocked down by some perfidious caitiff; at length, finding all resistance fruitless, I defended my head as well as I could, with my violoncello, and lay in patient expectation of their exhausting their brutal fury upon me. The whole band then moved on to slow music, and every individual, as he past by my vehicle, left me some token of his resentment: one pelted me with carrot-tops, turnip-parings, cabbage-stalks, dandelions, water-cresses, and all the ordure of the green market; another endeavoured to sepulchre me with the most odious remnants and productions of the animal reign; such as pigs-paunches, dead cats, rotten puppies, the tripe of a dead horse, and various other matters which decency prevents me from relating. Nay, to such a pitch a pitch of madness were they arrived, that they emptied three pots of urine upon my defenceless head, which I was afterwards told, but this I cannot report for certain, had been filled for that very purpose, by the freeholders in the country interest.

I very luckily received no other damage than the daubing my clothes from this terrible adventure; and therefore, as soon as I had an opportunity of escaping, I descended softly into the croud, and was leaving a town where I had been so unjustly persecuted with great indignation, when I was kindly invited in by the landlord of the *Hog in Armour*, which invitation, in my present unhappy condition, I did not chuse to decline. He had been witness to my cruel treatment, and imagined I had suffered for my adherence to the opposite party, to which he was strongly attached himself; nor did I think proper to undeceive him. He very kindly carried me to his pump, and pumped

upon me with his own hand, till I had regained my former purity, both in refpect to fight and fmell: he then placed me by his kitchen fire, filled me out a glafs of gin, and bade me be of good courage. I replied that I was not fo much exafperated by any perfonal injury which I had received, as mortified at the falfe ideas I had entertained of the inhabitants of this town, who had been reprefented to me as extremely polifhed, and great proficients both in the theory and practice of mufic, particularly the *" Carillon fci-*
" ence; concerning which I had determined to inform myfelf in a particular manner."

He told me I muft not be out of humour with his townfmen, who were at bottom a plain, honeft, good-natured people; "and" added he with a look of myftery, "I am fure they never would have proceeded to thefe extremities, had they not been fet on by fome officious, intermeddling perfon." I begged he would

explain

explain himself, upon which he asked me, If I had not observed a tall, thin, hungry, knock-knee'd man, in a grizzle-wig, rusty black coat, dirty shirt, and a thread-bare pair of green velvet breeches? I told him I thought I had, but could not be positive. "That fellow," proceeded he, " was formerly catch-pole to a
" bailiff in our town; but was turned off
" for want of courage and dexterity; he
" then commenced pimp and bully to a
" bawdy-house, but had not address
" enough to succeed; however, after va-
" rious metamorphoses, I hear he is re-
" tained by a London bookseller, to write
" a certain Grub-street journal, published
" monthly and called a *Review*. When-
" ever we have any dirty work to be
" done, such as scurrilous libels, electi-
" oneering lies, ballads, or addresses to
" the freeholders; any thing, in short,
" which requires knavery, effrontery, and
" a skin which must be cudgel-proof, we
" have him down from London at the

" rate

" rate of half a crown a day, and his
" beer. Now as this fellow values him-
" self not only upon his literary talents,
" but also upon singing a good song, and
" being a tolerable bow-hand, I cannot
" help thinking that he was instigated
" by a jealousy of your superior talents
" to misrepresent you among the free-
" holders *. For though I was at too

" great

---

* Not content with this unprovoked and cruel treatment of me, the hackney author above aluded to, has since the publication of my Travels, endeavoured to do me still further mischief by his pen. I have, indeed, every reason to despise the attack, as it is contained in a publication, which I am well informed few persons read, and fewer still pay any attention to; and as it is very evident, that of the multiplicity of books which its authors pretend to give a character of, they have never seen one half, and do not understand the other: yet had the critics confined themselves to reflections upon my understanding and behaviour, I should have kissed the rod; for I too well know the disadvantages of my education, which indeed are common to me with all other musicians, to think I could produce any thing which would not be liable to a thousand very just objections and criticisms. Indeed as to that particular, I am very conscious of the defects of my great original itself; but I comforted myself by reflecting, that a musician was not obliged to be a scholar, or a man of sense; and that no one could justly reproach my productions for being silly, frivolous, and uninteresting,

without

" great a distance to judge of your me-
" thod of taking *Appogiatura*, yet I could
                                    " plainly

without obliquely wounding those of the great Doctor himself. But the calumny which chiefly affects me, and which is the only one that I should think worthy my notice, is that of being a secret enemy of the illustrious personage whom I so much admire; and having maliciously endeavoured to satirize the celebrated singing and dancing Tour to the Continent. To have the genuine sentiments of my heart mistaken, or misrepresented, and to be accused of writing a lampoon, where I meant to express the sublimest panegyric, is a mortifying circumstance, and must deeply wound a man of any sensibility; although to be abused and misunderstood, is a misfortune common to me with the best authors both of ancient and modern times. But as to the accusation of malice, I trust that nothing can appear more palpably absurd, (except the above misrepresentation of my character and principles) and the gentlemen who have urged it against me, would have done well to consult the dictionary, before they attempted to write. It is malice to ransack a person's private life, and to publish the little inadvertencies which his passions or his temper have led him into, with a design of injuring his reputation, or his fortune. It may be also termed malice, when the unfortunate particularities of a man's voice, or figure, are exposed to the public, with a view of rendering him ridiculous; though this talent constitutes the chief merit of a certain celebrated buffoon, who has long directed the laughter, and guided the taste of the British nation. Again, when the effusions of human weakness, intrusted to the indulgence of private friendship, are posted up to gratify vulgar curiosity; this may I think be justly accounted malice, though it has been the practice of very great patriots, and
                                                                very

"plainly discern that your sinfonies were full of light and shade, your accompaniments ingenious and transparent, and your

very great philosophers. But to burlesque, controvert, or criticise works, which are voluntarily exposed to all mankind, and whose author could have no other motive for their publication than the opinion of his own superior abilities, argues no more of this ungenerous disposition than a man's criticising a picture at an exhibition proves him to entertain a personal antipathy to the painter. If the ridicule and opposition be unjust, they may indeed prove the weakness and ignorance of their author, but can never subject him to any other censure; if he has confined himself to the work, without attacking the private life, or unpublished sentiments of the writer; if on the contrary they be just, he does an essential service to the public, by preventing the adoption of improper models, either in style, or manners, or opinions. Had I really therefore written with a design of ridiculing the Doctor, which I think none but reviewers will impute to me, those gentlemen should have been the last to brand me with the epithet of malicious, who scarcely procure a wretched subsistence by waging a periodical war with almost the whole tribe of authors. With respect however to another part of their criticism, I confess that I should not once have introduced the disagreeable necessities of our nature, however important to my narration, had I not observed that the great man to whom the British nation owes its new system of morality, as well as great improvements in the theory of dancing, had not only a fine taste for all the graces of person and manner, but the most accurate nose (owing perhaps to his accomplished manner of blowing it) of any gentleman in the Feu de Foies, for distinguishing perfumes; which circumstance

" *your poetry much heightened by the rich*
" *and varied colouring of your instrument.*"

I answered, that I was obliged to him for his favourable opinion of my poor abilities, and very much inclined to admit the apology he had made for his townsmen; for, as I told him, I was very sensible that the mere intoxication of beer and liberty, rarely produced such excesses as I had experienced; and that in all countries, even the most refined and musical, where neither a drop of beer, nor a spark of liberty was to be found, public processions were apt to excite rioting and licentiousness among the vulgar †.

At this time three dancing bears were brought into the yard, which my landlord running out to accommodate, put an

---

stance his fair editress has thought too interesting to the public to expunge it from her useful collection *.

* *I must not omit too, that when he breaks wind he smells exactly like Sultan.* Lord Chesterfield's Letters, Vol. iii Letter CCLXVI.

† This procession seemed to have been as much the occasion of riot and debauchery among the common people, as the beer and liberty with which an English mob is usually intoxicated on a rejoicing night in London.

TOUR THROUGH GERMANY, &c.

end

[80]

end for the prefent to our converfation *. The bears immediately began a ferious dance, and to oblige my friend and the company, I played to them upon my violoncello, and muft confefs they performed their movements with great eafe and exactnefs; *Bruin*, the firft man-bear, "had "great force and neatnefs, and a gentle- "man's fervant who ftood by affured me "that he equalled *Slingsby* in his *à plomp*, "or neatnefs of keeping time; and that "the Bruini's *many twinkling feet* and "breafts were not inferior in agility to "thofe of Signora *Hidou*." During the dance, the fecond man-bear (a very young performer) a little alarmed the company by difplaying too much fenfibility; for having a very quick and fine ear, while I was playing in a ftrain fomewhat *amorofo*, he fuddenly caught hold of a pretty young

---

* At this time fome wild beafts were brought to the palace gates, which all the company running to fee, put an end for the prefent to our converfation.

TOUR THROUGH GERMANY, &c.

woman

woman standing near him, and locked her between his fore-legs in so strict an embrace, that she screamed out, and the *ballet-master* was obliged to have recourse to blows before he could oblige his scholar to quit his hold, and I am confident that it was owing more to my changing the measure, than to his cudgel, that they were disengaged at last. Bating this *faux pas* however, the performance was not only decent, but "*the story of the dance well told;*" and as the same gentleman's servant observed (who, by the bye, seemed to have a great deal of taste, and said he had often kept his master's places at the Opera-house,) had these performers worn hoops, they would have greatly resembled the majestic petticoat heroes of that splendid theatre.

Having taken a polite leave of my friends the publican, the ballet-master, and his bears, the next place I visited was
BIRMINGHAM,
A most noisy, unharmonious, smoaky town,

town, where the harsh sound of the hammer and anvil, together with the incessant clashing of pots, frying pans, and coppers, which was the only music I heard at my arrival, made me augur ill of my success at this place. However, I was well informed that it had lately been the seat of oratorios, and the receptacle of the *castrati*, that its inhabitants had studied oratory under the tuition of the celebrated Mr. *Herries*, that they were moreover honoured once a year by the presence of the manager of the Opera-house at London, and, if I mistake not, had even heard Lord S. himself play upon the kettle-drum at their music-meeting. I resolved therefore to make my arrival known; for which purpose (as I had no recommendatory letters to any person here) I employed the town-cryer *, for a

* " I sometimes wished to employ the town-cryer at my first entrance into a city, to tell the inhabitants who I was, and what I wanted; for it frequently happened, where his majesty had no minister, that I was on the point of quitting a place before this was known."

TOUR THROUGH GERMANY, page 89.

mug

mug of ale, to proclaim my name, profession, and place of abode, through every street; and withal to give notice, that my stay there would be but short. This proclamation soon produced an enquirer after me; he directed me to the house of a gentleman, who, he said, he was sure would be glad to see me, being at that time in great want of a music-master for his daughter. I immediately waited upon the gentleman, who was an elderly person of a very severe and suspicious aspect. He roughly asked me what was my business? to which I answered, that my profession was music; and added, that I had a new and very expeditious mode of teaching to play on the harpsichord, *forte piano*, and organ; by which I would undertake to give any young lady of tolerable parts, a *shake* in two lessons, and a *swell* in three. As soon as I had said this, he very abruptly quitted the room, where I waited some time expecting the entrance of his daughter, whose harpsi-

chord I began tuning, preparatory to my first lesson. But while I was thus employed, four fellows came up to me, and without any ceremony dragged me out of the room into the yard. When I enquired the meaning of this rudeness, one of them told me, his master wanted to see me dance; I replied, that I did not profess dancing, but music; and that there must be some mistake in the business;—the gentleman himself now appeared, followed by another servant who carried a blanket. " Now, Mr. Music-
" master, said he, with a malicious smile,
" my servants shall shew you a much better
" shake than you ever taught a scholar in
" your life." The men immediately placed me in the blanket, which they held by the corners, and tossed me about in it in a most severe manner, till their strength was exhausted, and then fairly kicked me out of the house. Enraged and mortified at this unforeseen and unprovoked outrage, I was almost determined to quit
this

this savage country, renounce all intercourse with my species, and retire, like *Orpheus,* to the woods and desarts. This resolution I communicated to my landlord, who dissuaded me from so rash a project, and greatly disarmed my fury, by informing me what was the true motive of the unaccountable behaviour I had just experienced; which it seems was owing to this gentleman having lost his only daughter, a very rich and beautiful heiress; who had eloped to Scotland the week before with her music-master, to whom she was since married. This circumstance appeared such a sufficient apology, that I again became reconciled to mankind, and pursued my intended tour with wonted alacrity, singing *adagios* all the way I went.

WORCESTER.

Here another mortifying circumstance occurred. As soon as I entered this ancient and magnificent city, I heard a sound more grating to my ears than all the tinkering of kettles I had left behind me. It was *a rude and barbarous flourish* of marrow-bones and cleavers, at the elevation of Sir *Watkin Lewes* in king Alfred's chair *. Seeing another election, another knight, and another band of sturdy patriots approaching, my mind misgave me, that there was also another, or the same reviewer in *petto*, to lavish his favours upon me, and finish the triumphs of the day. I was resolved therefore to depart without beat of drum, and to proceed directly to *Bristol*; and shall wait to deliver the letter which Dr. *Smirk* favoured me with to Dr. *Demisemiquaver*, till a more convenient opportunity;

" When the hurly-burley's done,
" When the battle's lost and won."

For I fear it is a serious truth, and my own experience has, in some measure,

---

* " A rude, and barbarous flourish of drums and trumpets, at the elevation of the host."

TOUR THROUGH GERMANY.

confirmed

confirmed it, that the wild notes of liberty, and the quavering of Italian airs, can never be heard together in concert *.

Had I been rich, I should have agreed with a coachman, who was just then setting out, and offered to carry me and my bassoon, in the basket, for six shillings. But as riches are not always the companions of genius, I rather chose to take my place in a coal-vessel, which was to arrive at that city in two days. Here, as the weather was extremely fine, I travelled very agreeably for the first day, and dined upon bread and cheese, and cold bacon, without making any observations

---

* " The fine arts are children of affluence and luxury; in despotic governments they render power less insupportable, and diversion from thought is perhaps as necessary as from action. Whoever therefore seeks music in Germany should do it at the several courts, not in the free imperial cities, which are generally inhabited by poor industrious people, whose genius is chill'd, and depressed by penury, who can bestow nothing on vain pomp and luxury, but think themselves happy in the possession of necessaries. The residence of a sovereign prince on the contrary, besides the musicians in ordinary of the court, church, and stage, swarms with pensioners and expectants."

TOUR THROUGH GERMANY, page 116.

worth

worth communicating to the public, except that I saw a man upon the bank angling for dace, notwithstanding the earliness of the season. The second day, as the wind suddenly changed from the West to the North-East, was foggy, rainy, and so exceedingly cold, that for want of Dr. *Burney's* lousy blanket*, I slipped my legs into a coal-sack, while I defended my head by thrusting it into my viol-case, which I tied under my chin with a pair of green worsted garters that my spouse had knit, and made me a present of during our courtship. We stopped about two o'clock at a little village on the banks of the *Severn* to dine; and here I cannot but inform the world, that Mr. *Bangor*, at the sign of the *Goat in Boots*, is an extremely civil and polite landlord, and has no contemptible taste in music. When I informed him of my design in making this expedition, he very obligingly led me into his hall, which

* See Tour through Germany.

was stuck round with various antique pieces of music, such as *Chevy Chace, The Children in the Wood, Three Children sliding on the Ice, The History of St. George,* &c. which he kindly permitted me to enrich my collection with. I begged hard that he would permit me to prick out the notes of an incomparable whistle as he performed it, which at length with great difficulty he complied with, upon condition however that I should not print it. But I was more than all surprized and charmed with his generosity, in slipping a piece of fried cow-heel into my pocket, and insisting upon treating me with a dram, before I went into the cold.

As I walked down to the river side, I remarked a boy, who was humming the tune of *Yanky Doodle;* and as I knew this to be an extremely popular air in some parts of *America,* I conjectured that this part of *England* was originally peopled from that continent.

Late the next evening we arrived at the large and populous city of

BRISTOL,

More famous for its commerce, manufactures, and such trifles, than for its taste in music. They have but lately had a regular theatre established there to civilize and polish the uncouth manners of the dissenters, who would even have succeeded in the savage opposition they made to this salutary measure, if the bishops had not espoused the cause of the fine arts. I have little doubt, therefore, that they will soon find that " *music is so com-* " *bined with things sacred and important,* " *as well as with our pleasures, that it* " *seems necessary to our existence:*" they will then quickly become friends to organs, and next to operas. As I approached the city, I was gratified with seeing the principal battalions of the militia, who made a most formidable appearance, and marched in exact time to the mar-

row-bones and cleavers. I put up at the *Dog's Head in the Porridge Pot,* and after powdering my wig with some flour, clipping my beard with a pair of scissars, and turning my shirt, I went to wait on Signor *Manselli,* to whom I had letters of recommendation. When I had knocked at the door, and enquired whether the Signor was within, I was informed that he was, but that I could not see him, as he was then busied in performing his vocalities. This answer, you may be sure, redoubled my curiosity, and I replied, " if a poor, yet I trust,
" not unknown musician, may be judged
" worthy of being a private observer
" of the Signor's meditations, I promise
" not to interrupt his reveries, and per-
" haps the Signor himself will not be
" displeased at your introducing to him a
" *Collioni!*"

When he learned that I was a musician, he bowed respectfully, and desiring me to pull off my shoes, as he did himself, he
led

led me to the Signor's apartment. When we came to the door, the servant desired me to pull off my coat, waistcoat, and wig, and creep through a hole, which he shewed me at the bottom of the door, as he assured me the Signor did not suffer even crowned heads to approach him in these moments of enthusiasm, without taking those precautions; " and sir," said he, " you need not think this an humili-
" ating situation, as I have seen many per-
" sons of the first fashion, among whom
" were several pregnant ladies, submit to
" the same ceremony."

I did not hesitate a moment to comply with the customary *etiquette*, but stripping myself to the shirt, I crept into the room with the same awful silence with which the ancient priests approached the Tripod of their God. Having posted myself behind a large screen, I beheld the Signor extended on his belly, while two young and beautiful ladies were gently stroaking his back with the palms of
their

their hands. He lay for some minutes pensive and silent, as if waiting for the inspirations of the divinity. At length, on a sudden, " his eyes were fixt, his " underlip fell, and drops of effervescence " distilled from his whole countenance*." Immediately explosions of the most musical intonation I had ever heard, issued from behind, and enraptured the whole company. After this, he successively coughed, sneezed, hiccupped, eructated, squeaked and whistled in the most harmonious manner that can be conceived. "Thank heaven," cried the Signor, " my " powers of harmony are yet undiminish- " ed: I shall still live to bless the world, " and polish this brutal nation." Saying this, he took up his fiddle, and played a most divine solo. I heard him for some time in silent ecstacy, till at length incapable of suppressing my emotions any longer, I precipitated myself into his arms, crying or rather blubbering out in

* Tour through Germany.

imitation

imitation of the great *Caffarelli**, Bravo! bravissimo! Mansclli, è Collioni, che ti lo dice. The Signor seemed somewhat surprized at my abrupt introduction, but at length, recollecting himself, he received me with ineffable politeness. The ladies at my appearance, had shrieked, and left the room, which in the first hurry of our embraces we had not perceived. But presently the Signor, glancing his eye downwards, recollected himself, and said with some warmth and emphasis, " O,
" fye, Signor *Collioni,* I took it for granted
" you were one of us." I blushed at the imputation, and said, " I hoped this de-
" fect would not lessen me in his esteem,
" as my country was not yet sufficiently
" civilized to have adopted the custom;
" and though some of our prime nobility
" had had the spirit and taste to lead the
" way, yet in the gross conceptions of
" the *English,* there was a certain degree
" of ridicule annexed to it, which de-

* Tour through Germany.

" terred

"terred several men otherwise of the "most exquisite politeness from submitting "to it." The Signor was kind enough to admit my excuses, but lamented this as the greatest obstacle to the national advancement in the science of music. However, he averred that several *English* young noblemen of fortune had to his knowledge undergone the operation in *Italy*, "and though," added he, "an ordinary "proficient may be exempted from the "practice, yet it is indispensibly necessary "for one who would fathom all the "mysteries of the art, to emulate the "illustrious names of *Senesino*, *Farinelli*, "*Tenducci*, &c."

I confess I was much staggered at what he said, more especially as I began to entertain some doubts myself whether the characters of a man and a musician were at all compatible.

I hinted to him, that I had formerly heard that a certain great Personage, *tàm Marti quàm Mercutio*, equally illustrious

lustrious for his martial and his musical talents, had adopted the practice; but as the Doctor had not recorded it in his tour to *Potzdam*, I imagined the report was without foundation.

"Ah!" said he, " depend upon it, tho' the Doctor has indeed omitted this circumstance in the admirable description he gives of that hero, and Dilettante practising his *solfeggi* at *Potzdam*, yet he would never have been either the monarch, or the flutist he is without it. Do you think, added he, that illustrious philosopher could amuse himself so calmly in his closet with *fugues* and *adagios*, while ten thousand *Polish* widows, and orphans, are imprecating curses upon the head of their unfeeling destroyer, unless he had totally disengaged himself from every incumbrance of his sex and species?"

Here the entrance of the young ladies interrupted any further conversation on the subject. The eldest, his niece, who was called *Gluckinelli Inglesina*, desired me to sing, which I did in the softest and most unmanly tone I could exert, that I might not again offend. I asked her what was her real opinion of my voice? she answered me with the most perfect affability, that I acquitted myself tolerably well *considering*; though " she thought " me" (like *Handel*) " too ambitious of " displaying my talent of working parts " and subjects, and added that my *canti-* " *lena* was often rude."

I took an opportunity when I was alone with this young lady, to enquire if the *castrati* were much in vogue at *Bristol*, and if that operation could be safely attempted on elderly gentlemen; this young lady smiled at my simplicity, and assured me that the operation was safe and easy, and not so painful as to require any degree of resolution, and that the *castrati* were the favourites of the ladies, both married and unmarried. She advised me by all means to undergo the operation, as the Doctor had done in *Italy*, tho' his excess of modesty prevented him from boasting of it in his excellent treatise. She added, that she could not with safety love me, unless I would submit to this for her sake.

This declaration from a young lady for whom I now perceived I had imbibed the most ardent affection, gave me great uneasiness; that affection however was purely platonic and spiritual, for personal charms she had no more to boast of, that ever I discovered, than the *Mingotti* herself. Besides the disadvantage of a contortion in the ogle, vulgarly called a squint of the eye, and a very long red nose, she had a mouth, which tho' it opened from ear to ear, discovered to the eye nothing but a dreary scene of ruins; the sad remains of a set of coal-black teeth. There was yet another circumstance to disgust the sensualist, and deter him from approaching this Syren with an improper familiarity; and that was the great offensiveness of her breath,

breath, which was so violent, that any person not "*determined to hear, see,*" and smell "*nothing but music,*" might have thought it hardly atoned for by the sweetness of her voice. Yet none of these circumstances damped the ardour of my spiritual attachment, founded, as it was, upon a solid basis, the love of song;— it was embodied harmony, the tuneful soul which I adored.

The reader who is unacquainted with the difference between a gross sensual passion, and a sublime, harmonic sympathy, may perhaps be surprized when I tell him, that while I was thus devoted to the divine *Gluckinelli,* I was at the same time personally captivated by the corporeal attractions of a little black-ey'd Gypsy, the wife of a barber in the town, who often shaved me for a tune; yet did not these grosser feelings the least impair or abate my musical platonic love. I might perhaps be excused, were I to conceal the progress and issue of these different amours;

amours; but they are so intimately blended with the scientific part of my work, and were attended with such important consequences to myself in my professional capacity, that the narration will I doubt not prove of great utility to my brethren.— For it was no common temptation that deluded me; though Mrs. *Sharp-set* was abundantly handsome, I could have resisted the blandishments of beauty, if a desire of making dangerous experiments upon the power and effects of music upon female passion had not seized my brain. For I had taken notice, that the imagination of this young woman was exceedingly lively, and far out-stripped her husband's, who was a plain dull man with little fire or enthusiasm in his composition. I plainly perceived this in all her gestures and movements, but when I sung some tender sentimental air, her involuntary sighs, blushes, and languid attitude, betrayed too plainly the iritability of her nerves, and that fine susceptibility of soft emotions

emotions with which nature has endowed the sex. No wonder that in a rude, uncultivated state of nature as I then was, I caught the subtle fire from her contagious eyes. Ah! how often did I sing the *sweet passion of Love* without once thinking of my dear *Gluckinelli*; how often did she encore my *O how pleasing 'tis to please,* without the slightest recollection of her absent barber! Madly determined to pursue the fatal experiment, and observe the full effects of my art; I next sung " *Haste, let us rove, to the Island of Love,*" at which Mrs. *Sharpset* was greatly agitated and danced about the room. Then I played a rapturous voluntary " *produced* " *in the happy moments of effervescence* " *when my reason was less powerful than* " *my feeling;*" and at length I proceeded to such excess of temerity, as to tune up *Geho Dobbin, Murdoch O'Blaney,* and several other inflammatory compositions; and finding my mistress " *attentive, and.* " *in a disposition to be pleased, I became*
" *animated*

" *animated to that true pitch of enthusiasm,*
" *which from the ardour of the fire within,*
" *is communicated to others, and sets all*
" *around in a blaze, so that the conten-*
" *tion between the performer and the hearer*
" *was only who should please or who should*
" *applaud the most,*" till at length, not contented with " *shewing her approbation by*
" *coughing, hemming, and blowing the nose,*
" *she expressed rapture in a manner pecu-*
" *liar to herself, and seemed to agonize with*
" *pleasure too great for the aching sense!*"
for at last, overpowered by my quirking and quavering, and transported beyond all the bounds of prudence, Mrs. *Sharpset* on a sudden leaped into my arms, hung round my neck, and devoured me with eager kisses, such as I never tasted before nor since. What man, what emasculated god could have withstood such potent snares? Ah! my serene *Gluckinelli* had'st thou been there, these tumults had all subsided, the devil had not gained the intire possession of my mind, voice and instrument;

ment; nor had I needed the painful operation of the barber's avenging steel to bring my wandering spirits back to reason:—for soon, and in the midst of our illicit joys, the door of the chamber was forced open, and in rushed Mr. *Sharpset*.—— Discordant oaths and curses, and the look and voice of a Fury muttering an incantation to awake the dead, bespoke the injured husband, and scared us from the bed. He retired a moment to fetch the instrument of his revenge. Mrs. *Sharpset* escaped, but in an instant I saw him return whetting his keenest razor; and concluding, that he meant to cut my throat upon the spot, I fell down at his feet, and in an agony of fear and penitence, roared out such a MISERERE, as was never heard at the Pope's chapel in *Passion-week*. Alas! how did I wish for the genius of a *Gluck*, " *to paint* my *dif-*
" *ficult situation occasioned by complicated*
" *misery, and the tempestuous fury of un-*
" *bridled passions!*" But *Allegri* himself,

had

had he chanted his own MISERERE, could not have moved the fhaver's unrelenting foul, or foothed his injured honour up in arms, and demanding its victim! I tried a fofter ftrain, and fang in melting mood, " Let not rage thy Bofom firing, " pity's fofter claim remove," &c. but it was all in vain: ftill ftrapped he his inexorable razor, humming out a fong of *Bravura,* the fubject of which was the caftration of the devil by a baker; (which, by the bye, is a very curious ftory, whofe authenticity I muft enquire into farther at my leifure.) I immediately augured my approaching deftiny from the burden of this fong; and the *Cornuto* prefently gave me to underftand that my conjecture was well founded. Having been till now in a cold-fweat, and corporal fear of my life, I congratulated myfelf on this exchange of punifhment, as a fort of reprieve, and confidering that I had fome time fince refolved, like another *Graffetto*,*

* TOUR THROUGH GERMANY, &c.

to

to undergo the operation whenever I found myself bold enough for such a voluntary sacrifice; I plucked up courage, and with great composure told the barber, that a guilty conscience was a greater torment to me than any he could devise; that I sincerely regretted that my pieces had not been like *Schwanberger's*, "*full of* "*pleasing effects, produced by fair and* "*honourable means;*" but that to expiate the crime I had committed, and appease the anger of heaven, and the honest man whom I had so deeply offended, I would patiently submit to suffer the righteous sentence which his vengeance meditated on the peccant part. The enraged tonsor took me at my word.

* * * * * * * * *
* * * * * * * *
* * * * * * * * *

The first thing that came into my thoughts after I awoke from the fainting fit, into which the paroxism of pain had thrown me, was to try my voice in its improved state.

state. I accordingly sung *A Dawn of Hope my Soul revives,* and found my powers wonderfully improved, and my execution delicate, interesting, and full of effects. "Ho, ho," cries the barber, "I am glad to find you are so merry," and resumed his old tune of the baker and the devil. I told him I thought it unkind in him to insult me, and intreated him to convey me home, which he very readily consented to do, and soon afterwards began to apologize for the effects of his rage, hoping I would consider the nature of the provocation, and not attempt to take the law of him. I answered, that upon condition he would freely pardon his wife, whose fault was venial, as her virtue had fallen a sacrifice to the power of harmony, I would decline any hostile proceedings against him on my own account, with which condition he appeared satisfied, and we parted.—I was brought home on a mule, on which I rode sideways; and as soon as I alighted at Signor *Manselli's*

Manselli's I sent for him into my chamber, and accosted him as he approached with the following air, in singing which I exerted all my newly-acquired powers.

> *Bear, O bear me on a sudden,*
>   *Some kind stroke of smiling chance!*
> *From this land of beef and pudding,*
>   *To dear* Italy *or* France *!*

During my performance, the Signor appeared perfectly astonished, and at length seizing my hand with rapture, "welcome," he cried, " O son of harmony! it cannot " be longer disguised, you are a brother— " you are one of us"——then expatiating on the dignity and importance of the order of *castrati*, he desired me, if not too much exhausted, to sing again his favourite air, which when I had done he cried out with transport;—" *nec vox* " *hominem sonat!* *I can hardly believe it* " *is the same pipe! such a volume of voice,* " *such an open and perfect shake! such*

" *unclouded*

" *unclouded light and shade! such clear-*
" *ness, brilliancy, neatness, expression, em-*
" *bellishment, intonation, firmness, modula-*
" *tion, smoothness and elegance!* and then
" your portamento *is as round and tight*
" *as a portmanteau, and you take* appo-
" giatura, *as easily as a body would take a*
" *pinch of snuff!*"

I was greatly flattered by these encomiums, but begged he would forbear, and suffer me to retire to my chamber, for the sake of necessary refreshment and rest. He immediately complied, and sent up to me, Doctor *Sougelder,* an eminent surgeon and man-midwife in the neighbourhood, very expert in vocal manufacture *, and an agreeable performer on the *English* horn; who, having applied an excellent dressing to my wound, left me to sleep, and " *thus ended this busy*

---

* Among the singers there are at present fifteen castrati, the court having in i's service two *Bologna* surgeons, expert in this vocal manufacture."

Tour through Germany, &c.

" and

" *and important day, in which so much*
" *was said, and done, that it seemed to*
" *contain the events of a much longer pe-*
" *riod; and I could hardly persuade my-*
" *self, upon recollecting the several inci-*
" *dents, that they had all happened in about*
" *the space of twelve hours.*" By the kind
and skilful offices of Doctor *Sougelder*, I
was soon restored to my health and spirits; and my adorable Signora *Gluckinelli*
in a few days paid me a visit of congratulation, which she repeated every day
during my recovery. It was in some of
these delightful interviews I discovered
how deep a theorist she was, and how
learned in the science of sound. Among
other discoveries and observations which
she communicated to me, and which I
treasure up, and mean to preserve for the
benefit of future ages, she disclosed to
me her real opinion concerning that important subject the *shake*. She assured
me that it was " *practicable with time*
" *and patience to give a shake where nature*
" has

" has denied it; that she thought, the
" shake ruined ninety-nine times out of a
" hundred by too much impatience and pre-
" cipitation, both in the master and scholar,
" and that many who can execute passages
" which require the same motion of the
" larynx as the shake, have notwithstand-
" ing never acquired one*."—" There is
" no accounting for this," added that illustrious young lady, with a sigh, " but
" from the neglect of the master to study
" nature, and avail himself of these pas-
" sages, which by continuity would become
" real shakes."

During my confinement to my chamber, I have had leisure to extract the foregoing observations, anecdotes, and adventures from my journal, and which I present to the world as the first fruits of my undertaking. If they tend in any

* " Both Pliny and the London poulterers agree that a capon does not crow, which I should conceive to arise from the muscles of the larynx never acquiring the proper degree of strength."

Philosophical Transactions. Last Volume,

shape to promote the study and practice of music in this country, and by that means lessen our national reproach of being *The savages of Europe;* immersed in politics, philosophy, metaphysics, mathematics, and other sour and abstruse speculations, I shall have gained my end, and shall congratulate myself on having in some humble degree assisted the generous efforts of the great *Giardini, Burney,* and the governors of the *Foundling Hospital,* to polish and *Italianize* the genius, taste, and manners of the *English* nation.

As soon as I had perfectly recovered my health, Signor *Mansella* instituted a grand *Féte Champétre* to celebrate what he was pleased to call my victory over the flesh and the devil; and to crown the whole, the fair *Gluckinelli* was that day pleased to condescend publicly to avow her platonic harmonic passion for me; and to promise me in the most endearing manner, that if ever she entered into the holy state of matrimony, I should be her CE‑CISBEO;

CISBEO; in which character she was pleased to say, I should still have frequent opportunities of entertaining her, both with my voice, and my instrument.

THE END.

APPENDIX:

BY

NAT. COLLIER,

SCHOOL-MASTER.

YES!—I will discharge that duty which my consanguinity and friendship with the illustrious COLLIER, as well as his particular injunctions have imposed upon me; although my pen drops from my fingers, and my feelings, as a man, almost incapacitate me to perform the task of an author, when I find myself obliged to inform the civilized inhabitants of the world in general, and the people of England in particular, that that great man, and unparalleled musician, is no more! O death, thou unrelenting foe to human excellence, how hast thou silenced the sweetest bassoon, and unstrung the most harmonious fiddle that ever enraptured a mortal ear!

[*A*]

ear !—But alas ! Dr. *Burney*, and Signor *Giardini* themselves, must yield to fate, and join the great *Castrati* of other times! It is now no season to indulge my private sorrows, and therefore I hasten to gratify the public curiosity with some particulars relative to that mournful and important event.

Mr. *Joel Collier*, as may be easily perceived in his writings, was a man of a mild and inoffensive disposition, as well as fine taste, and exquisite sensibility. During his stay at *Bristol*, he had received some tincture of methodism; which accident, joined to the continual reproaches of his wife, a woman of little refinement, and a very disagreeable temper, seemed to have thrown him into an unusual degree of melancholy. But this apparent alteration in his manner did not much disturb me, as I thought the loss he had sustained might naturally diminish his vivacity, without injuring his health. At length, one day, after having exhibited his hand-

organ

organ at a country wake, he expressed some doubts about the lawfulness of playing any other than church-music; and begged me to bear him company in singing the 104th Psalm. This I readily complied with, but resolved to be very attentive to all his future motions.

The next Sunday, after having heard a sermon upon a text taken from the Revelations, he invited me to drink a pot of beer, and smoke a pipe with him at his own house. Mrs. Collier being absent, he took that opportunity to speak to me with great force and freedom, upon what he was pleased to call the levities of his former life, in a carnal state. He principally lamented his having been fiddler to the dancing bears, and having officiated in that character, at a celebrated school where grown gentlemen are taught to dance allemandes and cotillons. He said, that from his own experience, he could affirm, that these places were seminaries of debauchery; and did not doubt, that

[A 2] all

all amufements of the fame kind, though more fashionable and polite, were liable to the fame imputation. He fpoke with great indignation of a certain promifcuous club of gentlemen and ladies of quality, which he called an infamous and notorious brothel, where the fmall remains of decency and chaftity, which before its inftitution had fubfifted among the inhabitants of this ifland, had been interred; and he recollected, with infinite pleafure, his having once refufed to officiate as candle-fnuffer at a mafquerade. I was furprized to hear him talk in this manner, as I had always known him to be a contented, unmeddling man; wonderfully fubmiffive to his betters, as moft fiddlers are, and rarely reading the newspapers, but in order to find advertifements for new tunes. He then mentioned, with great contrition, the fin he had committed with the barber's wife at Briftol, but added with a figh, he hoped it was atoned for by the great punifhment he had undergone;

gone; and that he should hereafter be allowed a seat with the four and twenty elders of Israel. These words, and the looks that accompanied them, made me tremble for his reason, as I knew that faculty was ordinarily not very strong in gentlemen of his profession. His countenance, however, instantly brightened up, and he talked with great copiousness and resignation of the infinite benefits of castration, which he called Regeneration, and a new creature, a profitable loss, a source of celestial promotion, and a symphony of heavenly music to his soul. He would earnestly recommend it, he said, to men-midwives, dancing-masters, music-masters, and all other gentlemen whose professions expose them to continual temptations with the fair sex. By these means, he said, infinite disorders might be prevented, and the honor of many families preserved: for how is it possible, added he, that a lady, either single or married, should confine herself within the bounds

of

of decency, when to deftroy all natural delicacy, and to impart an artificial fenfibility, both to mind and body, is the avowed end of all prefent female education? Poor deluded Mrs. *Sharpfet*, was a fatal example of this; and he doubted not, that every town in England, which was infefted with fingers and fiddlers, and fuch vermin (as he was then pleafed to call them) could furnifh many fimilar inftances.

Though thefe fentiments were very juft; yet he inftantly added others, which bore the ftrongeft marks of infanity. He told me, that he intended, if the fale of his Travels fhould produce a fufficient fum to defray his expences, to pay a vifit to *Rome*, as he was pre-deftined to convert the Pope, and all the *Caftrati* of that city: and when I defired a tune upon his handorgan, thinking it might be a mean of compofing his mind, he anfwered gravely, that he would never play a tune upon any other organ than *Joachim Wagner's*. Here the converfation was interrupted by the entrance

entrance of Mrs. *Collier*, to whom I privately took an opportunity of recommending the health of her husband, and then went away. Two days after, as Mr. *Collier* was visibly declining, I sent for Dr. *Gruel*, a very famous physician in that neighbourhood, and to Dr. *Columbo*, another great medical writer, who was then happily upon a visit to the former. The messenger found one of these illustrious men stirring a decoction of hemlock, with a hemlock stick, as he so justly recommends in his excellent book about guts; and the other ventilating through a quill, with a certain natural machine, into a tea bason of lime-water, to evince the presence of fixable air in the animal *rectum*. These great men jointly prescribed, according to the principles of the new practice, hemlock and an aerial clyster.

On the Thursday following, I was, at my cousin's earnest request, sent for to his bedside, as in spite of the repeated doses of hemlock he had taken, his health became hourly

hourly worfe. I found him betwixt his two doctors, in the fituation of *Socrates*; one was prefenting the Athenian beverage, while the other was endeavouring to recruit the lofs of animal fpirits, by inflating the contents of fifteen ox-bladders, filled with fixable air; both the doctors affured me their practice was infallible, and yet I could not help forming unfavourable prognoftics of it, from the pale and emaciated looks of my kinfman. They received me with great cordiality, and entreated me to fing him two or three ftaves out of *Sternhold* and *Hopkins*, in which I acquitted myfelf very much to his fatisfaction; and, at my defire, the two medical gentlemen joined their voices. In the middle of this exercife, Mr. *Collier* happening to hear the chimes of the parifh church, ftarted up, and with great vociferation affirmed, they were the *carillons* of *Harleim*. I reminded him that we were in England, at an immenfe diftance from Harleim; he anfwered, he knew that

that very well, but that he had the gift of *second-hearing*---that's wonderful, cried I---Not at all, replied he, the second-hearing is only wonderful because it is rare, for confidered in itfelf, it involves no more difficulty than the *second-fight*, the Cock-lane ghoft, or the cogitative faculty. Here one of the phyficians, who is a tall, black man, with a pug-nofe, and wide mouth, defiring my coufin to compofe himfelf, he ftared wildly upon the doctor, called him the devil that ufed to dance upon *Joachim Wagner*'s organ, and afked him what he did there without Dr. *Burney's* leave? but in this his memory doubtlefs had failed him as well as his underftanding; for it was an angel, and not a fiend, which Mr. Wagner had fuperfixed to that excellent piece of machinery. The phyficians being fomewhat difcompofed at this extravagance, withdrew, and Mr. Collier inftantly becoming calmer, began a converfation about his own Mufical Travels. He faid, that what he chiefly regretted in this indifpofition, was his being difqualified for making thofe alterations in his work

[B] which

which he meditated, and that he sincerely lamented having bestowed so much time and labour upon such unprofitable vanities as prophane music, which he now was convinced was one of the allurements which Satan makes use of to entice unwary mortals to their perdition. For, said he, I have observed with very great regret, that among the higher class of people, this love of sing-song, and *fa, la,* always occasions a general depravity of character, and only subsists by the total neglect of every superior qualification. What has it produced in this country? our noblemen are become fiddlers instead of statesmen, and their wives and daughters have exchanged the modest and amiable qualities which once adorned them, for meritricious airs, and a meritricious conduct. The young women too of an inferior rank, instead of being taught one single thing, which might be useful to themselves, or advantageous to their families, are solely instructed in those arts, which our wiser forefathers imagined were better adapted to courtesans than to modest women.

women. Hence, added he, in a louder voice than could have been expected in his present state, libertinism is increased at the expence of honourable love, domestic discord invades the peace of families, fiddlers, opera-dancers, and hair-dressers stain the bed of nobles; and every disorder which is the sure forerunner of national destruction extends its ravages in this devoted country. Among the lower classes of mankind, what else has the taste for music ever produced but drunkenness, idleness, and dissipation? those whom nature intended to be useful to society as manufacturers or labourers, are elevated above their sphere; brought up to useless arts, and taught to prey upon that public, which they would have served or protected, had they been permitted to follow their original destination. And I would fain know what one advantage these destructive trifles have ever produced to any one nation under the sun? are not the Italians, from whom this pest has been originally transmitted to us, examples of the most disgraceful vices, as well as the worst government,

vernment, and the extremeſt poverty, (the inſeparable companions of ſuch frivolous ſciences) even under the mildeſt climate, and the moſt fertile ſoil of Europe? even thoſe Electors of Germany, for whom, added he, I have the greateſt reſpect, for their civil treatment of my harmonious friend, and their frequent preſents to him of jugged hares and veniſon-paſties, are in reality much fitter for caſtrati than princes. What is it to the miſerable ſubjects who ſuffer the accumulated evils of oppreſſion and poverty, while their gracious ſovereign is applying the whole energy of his genius to an *adagio*---what is it to them that a new eunuch is added to the ſcreaming tribe, who defraud them of the price of their toils, or that an Engliſh muſic-maſter is fed upon cold partridges, and admitted to hear their royal maſter warble ſongs of *Bravura?*

I had liſtened with great attention to this long harangue, which was ſo unlike the uſual converſation of my couſin, both in ſtile and ſentiment, that I feared his intellects were diſordered; but what followed

lowed seemed still more wild and incoherent. He told me, that he was afraid his Travels, which he protested were written with the purest intentions, might do much hurt in the world, by contributing to the present musical extravagance; but that, if he lived, he would make ample amends, by undertaking a second journey through England, in which it should be his sole business to enquire into the past and present state of the organ in every capital town and he was not without hopes that the pious Dr. *Samuel Johnson* might be prevailed upon to accompany him. For my cousin had observed, with great grief, that in many churches he had visited, part of the gilding had been sacrilegiously scratched off the organ; which he supposed was effected by the nails of the charity-children, who generally occupy the contiguous seats, with a prophane intent to decorate their gingerbread watches with the holy spoils. And although he was not so uncharitable as to wish, (in imitation of that great traveller to the Western Isles,) that the little pilferers might have no dinner 'till

till they had ate the denuded pieces, yet he treated the contemptible philosophy of the age, which winked at such impious practices, with as much poignancy and severity, by exclaiming that cathedrals were the only supports of true religion; that if bells, which serve to awaken the bishops; and choiristers, which lull them to sleep; were abolished, there would be no difference betwixt high-church and low-church; bishops themselves would soon be turned out of their stalls, and episcopacy being extinct, there would be a horrid chasm in the creation. He then, with great fervency, thanked God, that he had formerly been enabled to resist the temptation of a dinner upon roast-beef and plumb-pudding, to which he had been invited by the vicar of a country-church, but had declined, because, during the service, he had observed the parson omit bowing to the communion-table, and afterwards heard him refuse to bottle up the remains of the consecrated wine as a remedy for the hooping-cough.

Where

Where organs were wanting in his intended tour, he meant to give an accurate history of the carillons and church-clock. He confessed, with a sigh, that, in this particular, his natural presumption had so puffed him up, that he had dared to deviate from his great original; and yet, added he, with much apparent complacency, in no one other respect can I be accused of taking such liberties; for as to a single observation upon the soil, agriculture, manufactories, or government of any one part of the world which I have seen, my book is as unexceptionable as that of the Doctor himself. On the contrary, conscious of my insufficiency to produce any thing of my own, worthy the public attention, I have applied myself to the imitating, as exactly as possible, the three greatest works which the present age has given birth to; the Letters of a late noble Earl to his *dear boy*; the Musical *Tour* to the Continent; and the much admired *Tour thro'* Sicily *and* Malta. I told him, that he certainly could not have proposed to himself nobler models, either of
sen-

sentiment or composition. This, said he, is my comfort and support against many of the objections which I have heard made to my work; for although I confess my adventure with Mrs. Sharpset to have been contrary to religion, morality, and my own principles; yet who can blame me for relating it, when in the first most excellent work, he has seen a father exhorting his son to adultery, and instructing him in those gentleman-like arts, by which he may triumph over the chastity of a married woman, and effect the dishonour of a husband, who had received him with unsuspecting hospitality and friendship? I know, continued he, that several persons have blamed me for accepting the dram and the cow-heel from Mr. *Bangor*, as well as the fruit from Mr. *Brazen*, and his brother-aldermen. As to the latter article, I could not possibly divine that the pine-apples and melons were pilfered from the pittance of an alms-house, and the gripes I suffered in consequence of eating them upon a fasting-stomach, would

would have been sufficient atonement for a greater crime. But with respect to the charge of meanness in accepting presents in general, I have even there implicitly adopted the manners and opinions of my betters; for after having destroyed all kind of principle and honesty in his son; after having conjured him by all his hopes of preferment, to deceive every man, and debauch every woman who fell in his way; (which his lordship judging, I suppose, from his own heart, accounts a very easy matter) what nobler end does that right honourable moralist propose to his pupil, what greater honour or reward for all his hypocrisy, grimaces and graces; than that of becoming the dependant of some minister, or some minister's mistress?

I said, his observations were perfectly just, that the book he mentioned was deservedly esteemed in this nation, as containing the only system of morals and education adapted to people of fashion, and that it must soon supersede all other works

works of the same nature, and be taught at our schools and universities; at which last I hoped to see a statue of the purest marble, expressive of the gratitude of the British nation, erected to the fair editress, who, with a zeal for reformation, which scorns the prudish scruples of decency, had, for the benefit of the younger part of our boarding-schools, translated into plain English, such high-flavoured sentiments, as his lordship's false delicacy had induced him to wrap up in a foreign language.

Many people, Mr. Collier said, had thought him guilty of speaking too much of himself in his own celebrated work; but he begged, if any accident should happen to him, I would inform the world, that this, so far from being the effect of his presumption, proceeded entirely from his scrupulous adherence to those two most finished accounts of travels the world has ever seen. Their ingenious authors, said he, have filled volumes by writing about

about themselves; by informing the world what they ate for supper, or breakfast; and whether they slept upon straw or a matrass. Nay, the Sicilian traveller is so fond of himself, that he cannot drop the subject even in the midst of a tempest; though I believe he is the first gentleman that ever wrote letters under the influence of sea-sickness. In another place, he envies the superstitious fooleries of the most ignorant of the Roman Catholics, merely that he may have an opportunity of telling the world, that he is a great philosopher, and then he ceases to be a great philosopher, that he may fill several pages with the history of a sprain in his ancle; tho' indeed he does not mention, at last, whether he rubbed it with opodeldock or arquebusade water, which I think is a great neglect in so accurate a journalist*.

As

---

* *After eating a hearty dinner with many friends at Mr. Walter's, and drinking plentifully of his excellent Burgundy, &c.* Tour through Sicily, &c.

As I was afraid he might injure himself in his present state of weakness, by discoursing upon subjects which visibly interested him so much, I begged him to compose himself. I told him that envy itself must allow his work to be a faithful imitation of his originals, and perfectly consistent with all the rules of writing acknowledged by the present age. Formerly, indeed, it was thought a work of some difficulty to become an author; visionary minds, imbibed with strange ideas of excellence, and prejudiced by reading pedantic ancients in languages no man of fashion at present understands, prepared themselves for this extraordinary character by long vigils, and emaciating labours; and it was thought necessary for a man to know something himself before he attempted to instruct others. But modern

---

All wrong—sick to death—execrable fierce wind, and directly contrary—vile heaving waves—   Ibid.
We had an excellent dish of tea, the most refreshing and agreeable I ever drank in all my life.   Ibid.

discoveries

discoveries have happily disincumbered us of these embarrassing constraints, and it is no longer in academic walks, or musty college-walls, or philosophical solitude, that the Genius of Literature imparts her mysteries to her votaries; but in opera-houses, at hazard-tables, coteries, masquerades, and every other place of fashionable resort. Is a lady tired of domestic employments, or thrown into hysterics by too assiduous an attention to her family?—she writes works of sentiment. Is an obscure person sent abroad with some raw youth of fortune to pack up his clothes, and prepare his breakfast?—he writes travels. Is some fiddler weary of officiating at boarding-schools, and directing the vibrations of young ladies' fingers?—he commences writer, deluges us with music, and fills large volumes with pompous anecdotes of superannuated castrati. Thus does our literature gradually receive the same improvement as our manners, and a perfect coalition is at length happily formed betwixt the fine gentleman and the author. That dogmatical ignorance which decides upon all subjects without having examined any; that petulant levity which skims the surface of sciences, without ever attempting to dive deeper; and that continual egotism which perpetually calls the attention of the company upon its own most trifling and uninteresting actions, are equally the characteristic of one and the other.

Mr. Collier seemed much pleased and comforted by these observations, and I, thinking repose might be useful to him, withdrew. The next morning I went to enquire after his health at 11 o'clock, but was told he had passed a very unquiet and feverish night. Upon my entrance into the room he raised himself in his bed, and told me he found himself so weak and faint, that he began to despair of his recovery. He said, that he had, contrary to the advice of his apothecary, taken some *Daffy's Elixir,* which had disagreed

agreed with him; but, he begged, if he should do otherwise than well, that Mr. *Hipps*, (which was the apothecary's name) might not be suffered publickly to impute his death to that circumstance; or to write a pamphlet against the use of a medicine which had been his *vade mecum* in all his journies; and had, in many cases, afforded him great relief. I assured him that no such thing should be attempted, for that I myself would take care to explain that matter to the world. After some further conversation he delivered to me his manuscripts, which he empowered me to make what use I pleased of. He then desired me, (as he said, he considered his situation to be desperate) to try that ingenious method of practice which is proposed in the Tour through Sicily and Malta. I accordingly assisted him in putting on a flannel, and after that, a silk waistcoat, which the squire of the parish was kind enough to lend him, to prevent the little sensibility which

which remained from escaping through the pores of the skin. I then repeatedly applied several shocks of electricity to different parts of his body, as the ingenious author and F.R.S. recommends, with a view to impart a supply of vital powers: he having not only discovered that Sir Isaac Newton was very ignorant of astronomy, but that the whole solar and animal system, together with the puerperal fever, depend entirely upon electricity*. But this experiment not succeeding, I desired Mrs. Collier, who had a very strong head

---

* See the admirable dissertation upon comets; upon he pressure of the air; upon the cure of diseases; and the treatment of pregnant ladies; together with several other philosophical discoveries, interspersed in the above mentioned Tour: particularly, a most curious account of *Archimedes*' burning-glasses, in which that great geometrician is proved to have hoisted the Roman gallies to the height of several thousand feet in the air, that he might have them " in a right line betwixt him and the sun," and then amuse himself at his leisure, by firing them with parabolic *specula*. It is no wonder that Mr. Collier should pay the greatest deference to the physical opinions of so universal a genius; but had he understood mathematics as well as he did music, his admiration would have been much augmented.

of hair, which had not known powder nor pomatum, nor even a comb for several months, to stand upon a cake of wax, while I elicited electricity out of her tresses, upon her poor expiring husband. To this she very obligingly consented, but without effect; for though she permitted me to try every experiment suggested by that truly philosophical traveller, together with some improvements in the method of combing, to which her husband's languid condition induced her to submit, I conld not perceive any visible alteration in the health of the patient; but this I attributed to the non-electric state of the atmosphere.

Mr. Collier then desired me to desist, and leave him in repose during the short time he had yet to live. He thanked me affectionately for my attention to him during his last illness. He recommended his wife and children to my care, whose circumstances, he said, he should lament, if he had not deserved too well of the public,

public, to doubt it's gratitude towards his family. He declared himself an enemy to all oftentation, and begged that no ftatue might be erected, at the public expence, to his memory; though, said he, should the parliament chuse to bury me in Westminster-abbey, near the tomb of *Handel*, I would not have my executors oppose it. He took that opportunity of declaring the most loyal and constitutional sentiments; and though he had been bred, like a certain high ornament of the law, in a wrong political persuasion, and had formerly picked up many a sixpence, by playing *Over the Water to Charley*, before that great man's door, yet, like him too, he declared he had seen his error, and was become a staunch Hanoverian; on which account he flattered himself, that should his lordship's nice-discerning eye, perceive any Jacobitical expressions in his works, he would kindly overlook it, and not persecute the printer with the flaming zeal of a converted renegado, who, to ingratiate

gratiate himself with his new friends, often over-acts his part; hoping to expiate his own former offences, by persecuting similar ones in others. For himself, he solemnly declared, that he died in charity with King William, and the promoters of the Revolution; and concluded by saying, that were the national debt five hundred millions, instead of one hundred and thirty only, he should consider it as a very cheap purchase of the inestimable blessings we enjoy; and of that most glorious period which is probably destined to introduce castration into the British dominions.

These were the last words which I heard from the mouth of that most excellent and illustrious musician; he died that very night, at a quarter past nine. After having put his few effects into the best order possible, and appointed him a decent burial in the parish-church, where he now lies undistinguished from the common dead, I hastened to indulge the public with another

another correct edition of his most valuable and instructive Tour; a work which will perhaps last, as long as sound taste and theory prevail in music, or a British audience be melted by Italian castrati. And I cannot help feeling a prophetic belief that when this nation shall cease to be formidable by its fleets and armies; when commerce, and honesty, and liberty, shall have abandoned us; when our statesmen and patriots alike shall be changed into pimps and fiddlers; and the whole science of government shall have become the art of extorting money from a corrupt and miserable people: even at that period, so immensely distant, (if one may judge from the present happy and contrary state of things) shall the name of COLLIER survive, and share the admiration of posterity with those of GUADAGNI and Doctor BURNEY.

THE END.

www.ingramcontent.com/pod-product-compliance
Lightning Source LLC
Chambersburg PA
CBHW030358170426
43202CB00010B/1417